T0286682

THE
TRAVEL
HACK
HANDBOOK

How to Make the Most of
Your Trip for Your Budget

CONTENTS

GETTING THERE & GETTING AROUND

HOW TO TRAVEL SMART

BEFORE YOU LEAVE HOME

HOW TO
TRAVEL SMART

Are you ready to travel smart?

Everyone wants to get the best out of every trip, but there's more to smart travel than just finding the cheapest prices. Savvy travellers don't just pay less, they get more – more rewarding journeys, more once-in-a-lifetime experiences, more memorable meals, more surprising stays, more cultural immersion, more wildlife encounters – giving more back to local communities and cutting carbon costs along the way.

The best travel hacks make travel easier and help you get more out of it. An overnight train ride saves you the cost of a night's accommodation and a day of travel time, but it's also one of the most immersive travel experiences, a chance to see the country through the eyes of its people, in a way that wouldn't be possible on an organised tour.

With travel costs rising after the COVID-19 pandemic, saving money is on everyone's mind, so read on for the best ways to travel smarter and cheaper, and arrive feeling fresh while everyone else is struggling to find their bags on the luggage carousel.

Travel hacks are not one-off tips, they're a way of life. Here are our top tips for getting the best out of travel.

≫⟶

A TRAVEL HACKS CHECKLIST

BE A MINDFUL TRAVELLER

"Mindful travel – thinking about what you are doing, why you are doing it and the impact it might have, while being open and attentive to everything that is happening around you – is a great way to get more from a trip."

Joe Bindloss, travel writer

SMART TRAVELLERS...

- Never pay more than they have to
- Travel at the best time, not just the cheapest time
- Book ahead so they're never disappointed
- Always have the right paperwork
- Travel light so check-in isn't a fight
- Carry digital backups of everything
- Seek out word-of-mouth recommendations
- Have authentic experiences, not manufactured experiences
- Buy a local SIM card and stay safe online
- Know the value of talking to locals
- Never run out of power or memory in the middle of a trip
- Know the scams and how to evade them
- See wildlife in the wild, not in a crowd
- Have travel insurance that covers everything
- Know the local transport hassles and how to avoid them
- See the most interesting sights, not just the famous sights
- Know when the festival starts and when to get tickets
- Take travel health seriously
- Know where their money is going
- Always travel responsibly

Six great reasons to travel cheaper & smarter

You could book a trip the way you always have – it's the easy option and it has never let you down before. Or you could try doing things differently, and enter the elite ranks of expert travellers who never pay too much and always get more out of every travel experience. Even if you follow just a few of the travel hacks in this book, you'll wonder how you ever got by leaving everything to chance!

Here are our top reasons to travel smart:

SAVE MONEY

It's not the only consideration, but with the cost of living soaring, who doesn't want to pay a bit less when they travel? There are many ways to save, from flying on a Tuesday to booking a room for before the school holidays. The rule is being flexible – if you must fly at peak times to the top destinations, you'll pay a premium and share the experience with a crowd, while smart travellers are enjoying a bargain break to lesser-known destinations down the road.

SEE MORE

By travelling smart, you'll spend less time in the airport, less time on admin and less time seeking out the things you forgot to pack; but more time touring temples, watching tigers and catching the perfect wave. Time is precious, so ensuring that it isn't squandered on needless queuing will let you get more out of a trip. Smart travel is about knowing what to do before you leave home, what can wait until after you arrive, and which things you can skip entirely.

MISS LESS

Who hasn't taken a trip to the right place at the wrong time, only to find the sights covered in scaffolding, the wildlife hidden by vegetation and the beach umbrellas acting as real umbrellas during sudden downpours? Knowing when things are open, the quirks of the climate and the best times for a bargain can make or break a trip. Time it right, and you could have the national park to yourself, or secure a seat at the top table in town without a battle.

TRAVEL DEEPER

If you rush into travel, you'll see the same things as everyone else, at the same time as everyone else. By travelling smart, you can visit the best sights, not just the most popular sights, and spend your time getting under the skin of the destination instead of queuing for a rushed glimpse of whatever the top sight in town is according to social media. Be open to alternative sources of information – tips from locals, messages on noticeboards, word-of-mouth recommendations from fellow travellers – and you may find your trip goes in a totally new direction.

TRAVEL SAFER

Trust the Scouts – 'Be Prepared' is a great motto for travel. By following some simple travel hacks, you can significantly reduce your chances of catching a dose of Delhi belly or losing your camera (and all those precious photos) to an opportunistic bag-snatcher. Being prepared will also stand you in good stead if you do get into trouble – taking out travel insurance (and knowing how it works) can make the difference between a mishap being the end of your trip or just a travel anecdote.

ESCAPE THE CROWDS

There's nothing wrong with sharing your travel experiences, but if your national park trip consists of 20 jeeps surrounding one exasperated leopard, you could probably have a better travel experience. Overtourism is a growing problem, and travellers are increasingly waking up to the merits of escaping the pack and seeing the places in-between the must-see sights. With some simple travel hacks, you can see the world's top destinations in a whole new light, while sharing the benefits of tourism more widely and preserving the best of travel for future generations.

BEFORE YOU
LEAVE HOME

Finding the right destination

Step one for any trip is picking the right destination, but there's more to this than sticking a pin in a globe. Visiting the right destination at the wrong time could turn a once-in-a-lifetime adventure into a never-to-be-repeated disaster. Try these tips for picking the perfect escape.

What makes the 'right' destination?

Travel brochures would have you believe that everyone wants the same thing when they travel: a pool, palm trees, a beach and some kind of goofy drink with an umbrella in it. Maybe you're not that kind of traveller. Perhaps your ideal destination is an empty desert or a gritty urban jungle? Match the destination to your real interests and you'll have a better trip.

Be true to yourself

Remember that you're looking for the right destination for you, not the right destination for everyone else. Do your research and be clear about what you want to get out of your journey. Think about what you really enjoy about travel and what you can actually afford – and you'll have a much more rewarding getaway.

What type of trip

Not every destination works for every kind of holiday at every time of year. Think about the kind of trip you're after – are you looking for culture or comfort, relaxation or adventure, company or privacy? Do you want space to breathe or the energy of crowds? Once you've answered these critical questions, you can identify a destination that fits.

Plan for the weather

Make sure the things you want to do are possible when you want to visit. 'Possible' isn't the same as 'enjoyable' – you can hike in torrential rain or hit the beach in a blizzard, but that might not be how you want to spend your precious holiday. Plan around the weather, whether that means making sure there are ways to keep busy on rainy days or heading to the hills to escape the summer heat.

Top tip

"My best tip for any traveller is to be honest about what you like. Everyone enjoys different things, so book a trip that fits your genuine personal interests, rather than being led by other people's opinions. And don't place too much trust in brochure pictures – find photos taken by ordinary people, so you can see what a destination is really like."
Joe Bindloss, travel writer

FINDING INSPIRATION

You don't have to start out with somewhere in mind. Spontaneity never hurt anyone, so look at all the options and be open to places you never previously considered. Here's how to discover your next destination.

Talk to people

You'll get plenty of recommendations from friends, family and colleagues – just remember that their dream destination might not be the same as your dream destination. Ask lots of questions to find out what the place is really like, and weigh up whether it's a good fit for your tastes and interests.

Go online

Google search terms such as 'best islands', 'top wildlife encounters', 'best places to surf' or 'most historic cities' to bring up list articles and overviews, and throw in the name of a region – Asia, USA, Queensland, Loire Valley – to narrow the focus. Use the term 'alternative' and the name of a place you're already interested in to find similar destinations you may not be aware of.

Be visual

Knowing what a destination looks like can be a useful primer for working out if you'll really enjoy the place. Try image searches on Google and Instagram to look at specific cities or places in a country that intrigues you. Browse for images taken by ordinary travellers rather than glossy PR or influencer shots.

Use the media

The travel press is constantly turning up new and exciting destinations. Browse travel websites such as lonelyplanet.com and nomadicmatt.com, magazines such as *Wanderlust*, *National Geographic Traveller* and *Condé Nast Traveller*, and the travel pages of national and local newspapers.

Read a book

Some of the best trips are inspired by books, from vintage travelogues by early explorers to local literature, so grab books about countries that pique your interest. If a particular story catches your imagination, consider a trip that recreates that journey – you can always change your plans, but it's great to set off with a sense of mission.

WHEN TO GO?

Deciding when to travel is more complicated than just picking the week with the best weather. Hitting the perfect spot on the travel calendar can be the making of a trip – and getting it wrong can mean arriving after the last wildebeest has hightailed it across the Serengeti. Try these top timing tips.

FAIR WEATHER OR FOUL?

The weather affects pretty much every trip, but it doesn't have to be warm and sunny 24/7. A little rain can cool down incendiary temperatures in the tropics, and it rarely pours down all day every day, even in the middle of the rainy season. Conversely, you might need particular weather conditions for a particular activity – scuba diving is best when water is clear, normally coinciding with drier, less windy weather.

BE EXTREME-WEATHER AWARE

Changing seasons can bring extreme weather conditions. The Atlantic hurricane season runs from June to November, while the cyclone season runs from November to April in the Indian Ocean and South Pacific, and the tornado season in the US runs March to June. The risk of extreme weather doesn't rule out travel completely, but you'll need an escape plan (such as insurance with evacuation cover) in case the worst happens.

KNOW YOUR SEASONS

The peak season usually coincides with the best weather, but this isn't a perfect measure of the best time to go. Peak season also means peak prices, frantic competition for accommodation and transport, and queues at the sights. Conversely, low seasons can mean limited choices, poor transport links and closed attractions. The shoulder seasons either side of the peak season often see weather that's almost as good, with lower prices.

BE CLIMATE-CHANGE CONSCIOUS

Increasingly, rainy and dry seasons are being shortened, extended or delayed by climate change, and flooding and summer wildfires are growing problems across the globe. This makes the shoulder season more of a gamble – you might get almost-perfect weather, or your trip could be a total washout. Do some research into recent weather patterns, and if you don't feel confident, adjust your schedule accordingly.

"You want to hit that sweet spot where the weather is acceptable and the crowds remain at bay. In Europe, that often means spring or autumn – May and September are usually safe bets depending on the location, but August is to be avoided – your destination will either be insufferably crowded because everyone chose to holiday there or mostly closed because everyone went on holiday."
Kevin Raub,
journalist and Italy expert

 ## CHECK THE FESTIVAL CALENDAR

Festivals can push prices through the stratosphere, leading to a crunch on accommodation and flights and a migration of people to rival the Exodus. The time to start thinking about accommodation for Mardi Gras in New Orleans during Shrove Tuesday is Ash Wednesday the year before. You'll need to think outside the box to secure cheap accommodation, whether that means couch-surfing or staying in the town down the road and commuting in by train.

 ## CLOCK THE LOCAL HOLIDAYS

Depending on your preferences, you don't want to be in Daytona Beach during Spring Break, or you really do want to be in Daytona Beach during Spring Break. The local holidays can bring huge crowds to places that are normally quiet, leading to gridlock on the roads and mobbed public transport. Check the school holiday dates before you travel – if you can't avoid them, expect shortages of family rooms and queues at family-friendly attractions.

 ## DON'T FORGET RELIGIOUS EVENTS

Don't rely on the local religious calendar aligning with the Gregorian calendar. Christmas and Semana Santa (the week before Easter) are busy in the Christian world, but many festivals are tied to the Hindu, Buddhist and Chinese lunar calendars, so the dates change every year. Be aware of the Islamic lunar calendar – it moves forward by about 11 days every year, and getting around can be tricky during Ramadan (Ramazan), the Muslim month of fasting.

 ## MIGHTY MIGRATIONS

Top times to spot wildlife are often linked to annual migrations. The Great Migration of wildebeest across the Serengeti in August is one of the world's greatest natural spectacles, and big avian migrations transform quiet coastlines around the globe into birding playgrounds, so plan your trip for when the wildlife is out in the open. Often, this is during the dry season, when the vegetation dies back and animals gather at shrinking waterholes.

WHAT TO BOOK

You could turn up without a reservation and hope for the best, but you might also find yourself hauling your suitcase from hotel to hotel after a 15-hour flight. Smart travellers book ahead for the important stuff to guarantee a slot, and to save compared with paying on the day.

The first night's accommodation

Even if you don't plan every stop in advance, make sure you have a comfy bed waiting for you on the first night. Email reservations are the easy option for an accessible record of your booking, and you can use Google Translate to get around language barriers.

Some rooms before you go

Your travel plans may not be set in stone, but having some hotel bookings in place is a sensible precaution. Websites such as booking.com, hotels.com and agoda.com often allow you to 'book now, pay later', and some hotels offer free cancellations or date changes until a few days before your stay.

Long-haul transport

As well as your first flight in, book ahead for longer journeys in your destination. The earlier you book domestic flights, car hire and long-haul trains, boats and buses, the lower the price and more options you'll have when it comes to operators, routes and seats.

Front-row seats

Reserving sights and activities in advance can help you beat the queues, particularly if you book 'priority entry' tickets. For big exhibitions or live shows, you might need to be on your laptop or phone the moment tickets go on sale. Museums and galleries often give priority to members – consider signing up.

Discount cards & passes

Special tourist cards for major cities can secure big savings, including on transport into town from the airport. Cards are normally available on arrival, but are cheaper in advance, particularly if you book online. Don't overlook annual passes for national parks (see p70).

Top tables

It's rumoured you need to book 10 years in advance to get a table at Damon Baehrel (damonbaehrel.com) in New York, but that's an extreme case. At most of the top restaurants, a few months should suffice. If you're planning a trip around a specific culinary experience, call ahead to find out how early you need to book.

Visitor-limited attractions

Some of the world's top attractions have strict limits on visitor numbers, so get in early to snag a slot. Only 3500 visitors are permitted to enter Machu Picchu every day, while Australia's Lord Howe Island only accepts 400 travellers per night. If there is a limit, check when booking opens and reserve early.

Time-dependent trips

Some things are only possible at a particular time of year – like seeing the northern lights in Iceland, or trekking to Everest Base Camp – so there'll be competition for flights, accommodation and tours. Check out your options six months ahead to maximise your chances of finding an affordable slot.

Trekking lodges & campsites

Lodges, refuges and mountain huts on popular trekking routes book out months in advance. To ensure accommodation on Réunion Island in peak season, book three to six months ahead; likewise for lodges on New Zealand's Milford and Routeburn Tracks. If you leave it too late, you'll have to camp.

National park accommodation

National park campsites and lodges offer full immersion in wild nature, but spaces are limited. Without an advance booking, you might end up staying miles outside the reserve, using half your time getting to and from the trails. Book ahead for national parks on long weekends and national holidays.

Inclusive travel

We travellers are a diverse bunch, and some of us have special requirements for a trip that need a little extra research and planning. The more questions you ask now, the fewer surprises will be waiting for you on arrival.

> "Don't let anti-LGBTIQ+ laws put you off visiting a country, except in the most extreme cases, such as Uganda, Iran or Saudi Arabia. Many anti-gay laws are remnants of colonial rule that have simply never been repealed and haven't been applied for decades. Even when that's not the case, foreigners are rarely targeted by law enforcement for being gay, so it's more about being discreet."
>
> **Tom Masters,**
> *freelance journalist*

LGBTIQ+ travellers

Everyone wants to feel safe and welcomed when they travel, so do some research on your chosen destination. Some places embrace LGBTIQ+ travellers with open arms; in other places, you might need to be more discreet. Make sure you know about local attitudes and laws relating to your rights – seek out LGBTIQ+-friendly accommodation and message the owners for insider tips on how the local scene works. The International Gay and Lesbian Travel Association (iglta.org) is a good starting point for information.

Travellers with disabilities

Travel can be complicated if you have a disability, so do your research. Finding an accessible hotel is just part of the puzzle – you also need to know how to get around at street level and by public transport, in case you need to hire a modified vehicle or have a person along to assist. Contact local disabled organisations for advice; specialist travel agents can arrange bespoke trips. Lonely Planet's Accessible Travel Resources (shop.lonelyplanet.com/en-gb/products/accessible-travel-online-resources) has more advice.

Older travellers

One obstacle to travel for older people is insurance, so shop around for the best deals. Specialists such as Allianz (allianztravelinsurance.com), World Nomads (worldnomads.com) and Saga (saga.co.uk) in the UK offer good packages. If you have special requirements, book ahead as accessible rooms and modified vehicles can be in demand. Investigate local discounts for seniors and check what ID you need. Seniors' organisations, such as AARP (aarp.org/travel) in the US, are invaluable sources.

A PRE-DEPARTURE CHECKLIST

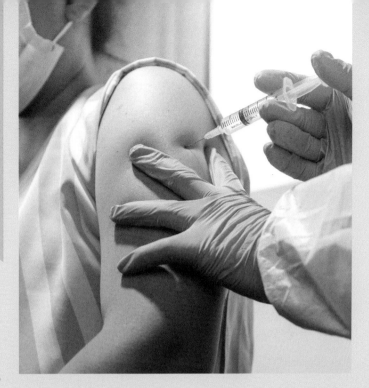

There's nothing worse than getting to the airport, only to discover that you forgot to check when your passport expires. Try these checks to avoid nasty surprises on arrival.

★ Check your passport

Thousands of travellers forget this essential detail every year. Always check when your passport expires – remember that you need at least six months validity from the date you plan to arrive in your destination, and often two spare blank pages for entry stamps or visas on arrival.

★ Check the visa situation

Again, super obvious, but always check the latest visa requirements, as things can change at short notice. Some places will let you in without a visa, some will give you a visa on arrival, and some require a visa before you can board the plane. Don't rely on the internet – confirm details directly with the embassy or consulate by phone.

★ Stay safe

Monitor the local media in your chosen destination in the run-up to your trip, so you're aware of any impending tropical storms, national strikes or contested elections that might cause problems when you arrive. Always check government travel advisory warnings, as these can affect your travel insurance.

★ Get insured

If you can't afford travel insurance, you certainly can't afford the costs if something goes wrong. Get a policy in place (you can even do this by phone on the way to the airport) and make sure it covers cancellation, healthcare overseas, repatriation in an emergency and any adventure activities you plan to get involved in (and keep the claim contact number handy).

★ Check in with the doctor

At least a month before you go, book a doctor's appointment so you have enough medication for any existing conditions, and get up to date with any travel jabs you might need. If you're in a rush, specialist travel clinics can fit you in at short notice, but you'll pay a premium price for vaccinations.

Visa hacks

"Never assume you can get visas in a third country while on the road. Many embassies only allow citizens or residents of that country to apply for a visa with them, and will redirect you to the embassy in your home country."

Tom Masters, freelance journalist

Always check by phone if you need a visa with the relevant embassy, consulate or high commission in your home country, at least a month before departure. Confirm whether you need to apply in person, online or by post – it makes a big difference to how long the process takes.

travel freely across the 27 countries of the Schengen Area using just your national ID card or passport.

Visas on arrival
Many countries offer visas on arrival, but these may only be available at specific airports or land and sea crossings. You may need to provide passport photos or pay in a certain currency, so check the details with the relevant authorities. Many land borders close overnight, so try to cross during office hours.

Applying on the road
If you can't get a visa for the next country on your itinerary at the border, you may need to detour to the capital city to apply at the relevant embassy or consulate. In some countries, obtaining a visa for a neighbouring state is a formality; in others, it's impossible – make sure you know the lay of the land before you set off.

Electronic Transit Authorities
Even if visitors are allowed to enter without a visa, many countries require travellers to apply for an Electronic Travel Authority (ETA) before travel. Apply online at least 72 hours before travel and carry a printout when you check in for your flight.

Passport essentials
Most countries expect you to have six months' validity on your passport and two spare pages on the date you arrive. If your passport is getting full or is within a year of expiry, apply for a new one a few months before you plan to travel (in case of processing backlogs).

Visa-free travel
Many countries offer visa-free travel to specific nationalities, but always check the terms and conditions, particularly the permitted length of stay. If you're lucky enough to be an EU citizen, you can

HOW TO TAKE A WORKING HOLIDAY

Some countries offer special schemes for young people, allowing travellers to work in another country for a year or longer, bypassing the usual red tape. Here's how to go about it.

Choosing a scheme

For most working-holiday schemes, the age limit is 18 to 30 (or 35), the visa lasts a year, you can only participate once, and only certain nationalities are eligible. The best-known schemes are in Australia (immi.homeaffairs.gov.au), New Zealand (immigration.govt.nz), Japan (mofa.go.jp), South Korea (overseas.mofa.go.kr), the US (bunac.org) and Canada (canada.ca).

How to apply

Applications are usually accepted six months ahead of travel, and you'll need proof of enough money to support yourself until you find work. Get in early, as spaces may be limited. There's normally a sizeable fee, and you'll need your birth certificate, character references and proof of a return flight (or the means to pay for one).

Hit the ground running

Before you go, look into the process for obtaining a tax number, applying for a bank account and other employment red tape such as the Responsible Service of Alcohol (RSA) certificate, needed to serve alcohol in Australia. Check if you need to apply for formal recognition of your home qualifications from the local authorities.

Where to work

Casual, seasonal work is the easiest to find, particularly in busy tourist hubs, whether that means fruit-picking in Australia, working at a summer camp in the US, or ski-resort work in Europe. Approach job agencies or enquire directly with businesses that need a regular or seasonal influx of workers, such as hotels, bars, restaurants and tourist attractions.

Have a plan

Remember, you aren't obliged to work every day that the visa is valid, so build in some actual travel into your itinerary. Many travellers save this until the final few months, to build up funds for the fun stuff. Remember to keep back enough cash to cover your living costs or a flight home if you can't find work.

Turn a business trip into a mini-break

Business travellers often complain that they only see the inside of the office and the plane. Turn your next trip into a mini-break with these work-hard, play-hard tips.

"My work finds me travelling all over the place, and I always ask clients about the best places to eat and drink and which neighbourhoods and sights they like to visit, and then follow their insights. A recent highlight was visiting the King Richard III Visitor Centre in Leicester; it was very moving and helped put a bit of work stress into context!"

David Marshall, CEO Marshall E-Learning Consultancy

 ## SWOT UP ON THE FLIGHT OR TRAIN

Unless you have pressing work to complete while you're on the journey, use your flight or train time to read up on the destination. Bring a guidebook, or go online and browse blogs, online travel magazines and, of course, websites such as lonelyplanet.com.

 ## USE GOOGLE MAPS

Before you leave, make up a Google map pinpointing locations you have to visit for work – offices for meetings, your hotel, locations for evening activities and the airport or train station – then identify interesting things nearby for any spare moments.

 ## USE GAPS IN YOUR SCHEDULE

You don't need a spare day to sightsee. If you've an hour between meetings, or a slot between the last of the day and an evening function, grab a rideshare bike and go for a cycle – even the CBD can take on a special character as the city winds down for the night.

 ## USE YOUR JETLAG TIME

If you find it hard to sleep or wake up extra early in a new time zone, use that time to see the place. Many cities come alive at night with food stands and street stalls, and most public markets are at their liveliest and most interesting first thing in the morning.

 ## MAKE EVENINGS MEMORABLE

Work events in the evening can be tiring and stilted. See if colleagues are open to shifting the meeting to somewhere more interesting – a casual work chat over dinner is more exciting in a buzzing hawker court or in the bar during the interval at a stage show.

TRAVEL IS BETTER SHARED

Travel agencies often charge supplements for solo travellers, and being the only passenger in a vehicle means covering all the costs. To save, gather your own travel group and split the bill. Try these hacks to find companions.

Use your contacts
Ask family and friends to see if they know anyone who's up for a trip. Friends of friends can make great travel companions, and you'll have the advantage of some common ground.

Ask the agency
Travel agencies may be willing to pair up solo travellers to create a double occupancy. You won't have total control over who you

travel with, but if you're flexible and sociable, it could be the start of a beautiful friendship. Also look out for packages for solo travellers from agencies such as Exodus (exodus.co.uk) and Intrepid (intrepidtravel.com).

Traveller noticeboards
Noticeboards in cafes, hostels and hotels can be great places to find travel companions. Look out for 'companions wanted' ads, or stick up your own with an email address or phone number where you can be reached.

Reddit
Reddit's Solo Travel thread (reddit.com/r/solotravel) does a similar job in the online space, and you can post requests for travel companions in the weekly

'General chatter, meetup and accommodation' thread.

GAFFL
Get a Friend for Life (gogaffl. com) is dedicated to putting travellers in touch with like-minded companions. Members are based in 190 countries, and there's a detailed verification process, so you can be confident about who you are speaking to.

Meet a local
Meetup.com is a great place to find locals with similar interests for activities, whether you're seeking a buddy to join you on a hike, or a second driver for a day trip. Women Welcome Women (womenwelcomewomen.uk) provides a global networking service specifically for women.

Staying safe

Every country has its issues, whether it's pickpockets on the Paris Metro or Australia's poisonous spiders. Try these tips to stay safe.

"If there's a natural disaster, like an earthquake or tropical storm; or a human disaster, such as a coup or a bank run, get straight in touch with your home embassy or consulate. They can only repatriate you if they know who you are and where you are!"

Joe Bindloss,
travel writer

Monitor the media
Check local news sites and the international sections of news sites at home, so you're aware of any issues in your destination. The website world-newspapers. com lists sources worldwide.

Ask a local
Always heed the advice of locals about any potential dangers, whether that's petty crime in the marketplace, riptides off the local beach or crocodiles lurking in the creek.

Know the law
Read up on local laws (see p124). Some countries have strict customs laws – such as the death penalty for drug smuggling – that you need to know about before you travel.

Your embassy
Note the details of your country's local embassy, consulate or high commission. They can't do much if you break local laws, but can help replace your passport and arrange repatriation in the event of a natural disaster or conflict.

The Tourist Police
Many places have special tourist police departments to take care of travellers. Find out how to contact them and store the details on your phone. If there isn't a tourist service, find out how to contact the local police in an emergency.

Healthcare
Research the local healthcare system – in some countries, private clinics are better than state hospitals. Take out travel insurance and check if you have to pay for treatments and claim later, or if the insurer will arrange.

GOVERNMENT TRAVEL ADVISORIES

Always read the foreign travel advisory notices from your home government, highlighting health, security and political issues, terrorism and crime, and areas that should be avoided. If a government advisory recommends against 'all travel' or 'all but essential travel', your travel insurance probably won't be valid. Comprehensive travel advisory services include:
★ UK (www.gov.uk/foreign-travel-advice)
★ US (travel.state.gov)
★ Canada (travel.gc.ca/travelling/advisories)
★ Australia (smartraveller.gov.au)
★ New Zealand (safetravel.govt.nz)

Staying in touch

Once upon a time, people thought nothing about being out of contact for a week while crossing the Atlantic, but these days, a few days of radio silence can raise anxiety levels. Always give some thought to the best ways to stay in touch with the folks back home.

PHONE CALLS

Don't make calls from hotel phones – use cheaper public call offices or free internet-based services, such as Skype, WhatsApp, FaceTime and Viber. Calling and texting on your mobile can be pricey if you rely on data roaming, so turn it off and use apps via Wi-Fi, or sign up for a local data SIM package. Many destinations offer tourist packages on arrival at the airport – see p120.

EMAIL

Increasingly, Wi-Fi is standard in hotels, cafes and even on public transport, so it's easy to stay in touch by email with a laptop, tablet or smartphone. But free public Wi-Fi networks aren't always secure; using a Virtual Private Network (VPN) or a local data SIM package can give you peace of mind. Ensure the network covers the areas you plan to visit and keep login details safe from prying eyes.

SOCIAL MEDIA

Make sure that everyone in your circle knows how to find you on Instagram, Twitter, TikTok, Mastodon and your other favourite networks, and set up a dedicated WhatsApp group so you can easily message your inner circle. Do live broadcasts via video-calling platforms such as WhatsApp, Skype and FaceTime to bring your people along on the trip.

WRITE A LETTER

Everyone loves receiving mail, and a letter from the road with some photos included will always raise a smile. Postcards are cheaper to send (and easier to write, as there's less space for text). Establish a correspondence using poste restante services as you go – just let people know the address to use (it's usually the main central post office).

TWELVE THINGS YOU NEED IN YOUR PACK

On your first trip, you'll bring everything but the kitchen sink. With a few trips under your belt, you'll narrow down the list to just the essentials. Here are our top 12 must-haves.

"By far my most-valued travel accessory is my pop-up mosquito net. This compact, collapsible item springs opens dramatically to sit atop your bed like a domed netted tent, offering you the safety of a cocoon. It's protection against everything, from dengue fever and malaria to the cockroaches, tarantulas, rats and monkeys that have managed to find their way into my room!"

Trent Holden, travel writer (@hombreholden)

1) A PORTABLE TRAVEL SCALE

It's always good to know how you're tracking against the airline baggage limit. Weigh as you pack and leave heavy 'might use' things behind, in favour of light things you can't do without.

2) A FOLDING UMBRELLA

Don't rely on being able to find a quality umbrella on arrival. What if you have to walk from the terminal to the bus stand in a downpour? A small folding umbrella keeps the sun off just as effectively as the rain, and it provides a bit of dignity in a downpour.

3) A SARONG OR SHAWL

Unless you're certain you can find one locally, pack a sarong or shawl. It's a blanket when the air-conditioning is icy. It's an emergency towel. It's privacy for getting changed on the beach. It's modesty when you can't enter a temple with your legs or shoulders showing.

4) SUNGLASSES

Shades look cool, shield your eyes and offer privacy; people are less likely to intrude if they think you may be napping. They're also perfect for subtle people-watching. Take quality glasses with UV protection.

5) A MUSIC PLAYER WITH HEADPHONES

There'll be moments when you want to shut out the world, and a music player with headphones means portable privacy. You could use your phone for music, but having something valuable on display isn't always wise – a cheap MP3 player is a better option.

6) A TORCH

Whether you're trekking off-grid or looking for your keys at the bottom of your day pack, an LED torch is a lifesaver. Bring a lightweight but sturdy model, and make sure batteries are easy to buy in your destination. Big cave-explorer-style headtorches are overkill – look for small models with button batteries.

7 PORTABLE SANITISATION

Antibacterial wet-wipes or hand gel are a bathroom in a packet, killing off germs on your hands before you dive into those delectable street-food snacks. It's your first line of defence again stomach bugs, COVID-19 and more.

8 EARPLUGS

Sounds are part of the magic of travel, but that won't always extend to the loud reggae on the bus or the pre-dawn call to prayer from the mosque by the hotel. Carry a few pairs of mouldable earplugs in soft foam.

9 ZIPLOCK BAGS

We're serious. Ziplock or press-lock bags are light and waterproof – ideal for organising stuff in your bag and keeping electronics safe when it rains. Keep a couple handy in your day pack for emergencies.

11 GAFFER TAPE

Having something that sticks to anything can come in handy for patching up a torn bag, mending a hole in your tent or holding up your mosquito net. You can even use it as an emergency sticking plaster. A small 2.5cm-wide (1in) roll should be up to most tasks.

10 A POWER BANK

Having the means to charge your phone or camera on the move could be the difference between cruising onto your flight and desperately hunting around for a wall socket so you can access your e-ticket. Look for power banks of 10000mAh or higher, ideally with USB-C connectors for fast charging.

12 A MULTI PLUG

Having multiple travel plug adaptors will only get you so far if there's only one wall socket in your room. Carry a multi plug so you can keep your phone, camera and laptop on the go, even if the only power supply is the socket for your bedside lamp.

© CAREPLUS

...AND FIVE THINGS YOU DON'T

If you're an everything-but-the-kitchen-sink packer, pause for a moment. A lot of what you need will be available when you reach your destination, and often for less than you'd pay back home. Above all else, avoid buying travel accessories at the airport, where air-side price hikes can be eye-watering.

1 Shampoo & conditioner

You don't need full-sized shampoo bottles weighing down your luggage. Carry travel-sized mini-bottles for those rare occasions when the hotel doesn't provide toiletries, or buy from a grocery shop or pharmacy on arrival.

2 Workout gear

That Lycra exercise gear is likely to go unused. Running shoes, shorts and a T-shirt is all you'll need for most exercise. One smart accessory is a lightweight fabric headband for keeping your ears warm (or the sweat from running down your face in the tropics).

3 Towels

When was the last time you visited a hotel that didn't supply towels? If you're trekking, a lightweight, quick-drying travel towel can be worthwhile; otherwise, use the towels provided by your accommodation, or buy one cheaply on arrival.

4 Pricey jewellery

Anything valuable you put on display is a magnet for thieves, so leave your diamonds at home. If you must accessorise, bring jewellery that's cheap and fun and doesn't look like it's worth stealing. The same goes for watches.

5 Superfluous shoes

How often are you really going to wear those towering heels or those brushed-leather brogues? What you need is comfy, sturdy day-to-day shoes or boots that can handle any walking, plus some sandals. If you get up to three pairs of shoes, you're one pair over.

Finding the right bag

Until scientists create a travel bag that expands infinitely then compacts down to fit into an overhead rack, you'll have to make do with the luggage available in the real world. The amount you pack will expand to fill the space available, so bring a smaller bag and save yourself the hassle of wrestling with a behemoth suitcase. Here are our top baggage tips.

Hold bags

In the hold, size is less of an issue so long as your bags meet the weight limit (usually 20kg to 23kg/40lb to 50lb per passenger). For easy manoeuvrability, pick a suitcase or bag with wheels (ideally a spinner case with four) and a tow handle. Chose an unusual colour, or add an identifying marker (a ribbon on the handle) to make your bag easy to spot on the carousel.

Backpacks 101

Your backpack is one piece of luggage you'll end up carrying yourself. For trekking, anything above 65L will become your nemesis as you struggle up slopes; pro trekkers try to stay below 40L. Keep things at hotels or in storage so you don't have to haul it all around.

Hard-shell or soft?

Hard-shell cases will protect your gear, but they can crack and you'll have to flip the bag open to access anything inside. Soft cases offer less protection, but they're easier to access, less likely to pop open and they can often be expanded by unzipping a flap.

Carry-on cases

A bag that fits into the overhead bins can save you big bucks on budget airlines if you skip putting a bag in the hold. Check the permitted size before you book, as rules vary. Remember, wheels and a tow handle will take up space and add weight.

"Everyone has their own favourite bag. For my cabin carry-on, I swear by the shoulder bags made by Crumpler (crumpler.com). They're almost indestructible, they have a padded pocket for a laptop and they close with straps and super-strong Velcro – it's really noisy, so you can hear anyone trying to open your bag in a crowd."

Joe Bindloss,
travel writer

Top packing hacks

Sure, you could toss everything you own into your case and jump on top to squeeze it closed, but your bag is more likely to arrive in one piece if you pack more judiciously. Try these top packing hacks.

Leave space

If you have to force your bag closed, the seams and zip or catch will be under strain for the whole journey, increasing the chance of catastrophic failure. Leave some space – you'll probably want to buy some things to bring home. To prevent things moving around, put something lightweight in the void, like a soft canvas shoulder bag or tote that you can use to carry fragile items in the cabin.

Two-stage packing

Pack in two stages – first set out everything you think you need, then make a second pass to remove anything that you aren't 100% certain you'll use. If you whittle the pile down by a third, you're on the right track. Other countries have shops, so leave out any heavy or bulky items that you can easily buy on arrival.

Wear the bulky stuff

Coats and sweaters take up loads of space, so wear your bulkiest items rather than cramming them in your bag. Planes and trains are usually air-conditioned, and if you get hot, you can pop these items in the overhead compartments without taking up valuable luggage space.

Fold, don't cram

Folded clothes take up less space than scrunched-up clothes. Items where wrinkles are less of an issue, such as T-shirts and tops, can be rolled up to save space. Use these soft clothes as a core, and wrap larger items around them, to reduce the risk of deep creases. When picking outfits, prioritise clothing that doesn't need to be ironed over high-maintenance fabrics.

Compartmentalise

You'll need a system to keep your bag organised. Some travellers use packing cubes – soft, lightweight, zip-up boxes – to keep similar items together. Others insist on lighter drawstring bags or compression bags. While they're less durable, press-seal or ziplock plastic bags will do the job at a push.

Heavy stuff goes at the bottom

Put shoes, books and other heavy or rigid items at the bottom of your pack – down by the wheels if you're using a rolling or spinner case. Keeping squishy items at the top will make it easier to tuck in extra things you buy during your journey.

Washbag tips

Your washbag is a booby trap – full of tubes and bottles that can burst open, dousing your toothbrush with cleanser. Consider sealing tubes closed with tape for the journey. Liquids are also heavy, and there's a 100ml limit per item for your cabin bag – other countries have toiletries, so take the minimum, and buy anything you need when you get there.

Personalise your bag

Almost everyone has a black suitcase. Make your luggage stand out on the carousel by choosing an unusual colour, or adding a colourful strap, tag, sticker, sew-on patch or ribbon.

Make sure your name and address are clearly marked so you can be reunited with your bag if it goes astray in transit.

Lock it up

Whether you use a soft bag or a case, make sure you can lock it up – theft of whole bags is rare, but items do 'go missing' from unlocked bags. Some cases have integrated zip locks, and many bag zips can be closed with a mini padlock. For a quick fudge, bind the zipper pulls tightly together with gaffer tape – remember, you're not making your bag impregnable, you're making your bag harder to steal from than the next bag on the rack.

Check the baggage rules

Everyone knows scissors and penknives go in the hold, but most airlines also insist that devices with lithium batteries (such as laptops, power banks and cameras) are carried in cabin bags to reduce the risk of fire. Similar rules apply for vaping devices and lighters, so pack accordingly.

"I keep my fold-up sleeping mat strapped to the back of my backpack, as it's bulky when rolled up and I get too lazy to use it if it's buried away inside. I like to keep it handy for laying down in airports, sitting on damp surfaces, padding bare train seats, and as a shield from overhanging wires and branches when riding on the roof of trucks."

**Mark Elliott,
travel writer**

THE TRAVEL HACK HANDBOOK

What to wear

Other countries have clothes shops and laundries, so you don't need to bring every outfit in your wardrobe.

★ Shorts

Don't go too short in more conservative countries. A pair that doubles as swimwear will come in handy, but many destinations insist on skin-tight swimmers for the pool.

★ T-shirts & shirts

Button-up shirts and blouses need to be ironed; T-shirts don't. Bring shirts with sleeves; many countries frown on exposed shoulders. Light, loose-fitting cotton shirts in light colours are the best option for hot countries (dark colours show off sweat marks). Prioritise casual shirts you can wear even when creased.

★ Fleece tops

Essential for cold and hot countries. They're light and warm and can fend off winter chills and icy air-conditioning. If it's cold and windy, bring a windproof jacket to wear on top.

★ Skirts & dresses

Quick-drying fabrics and loose-fitting styles are the way to go. Outfits that cover most of the legs are recommended for more conservative countries.

★ Underwear

Bring plenty. Socks and underpants take up hardly any space and you could be days from the next laundrette.

★ Jackets

A blazer is usually a liability, but a light waterproof and windproof layer can come in handy. For serious cold, down jackets can squish down to almost nothing in a compression bag.

★ Trousers

Jeans are heavy, bulky and take a long time to dry – bring lightweight cotton trousers with deep pockets that things won't fall out of.

★ Smart clothes

Some hotels and restaurants have a dress code for dinner, so a smart outfit can be useful – but it won't stay smart, so you'll need access to an iron.

★ Shoes

Two pairs are plenty – ideally, one comfy pair and some sandals. Only bring posh footwear if you absolutely can't get away with your comfy day shoes.

RECORDING YOUR TRIP

Think in advance about how you plan to record your trip. You may already be carrying a lightweight camera and video camera in the form of your smartphone – so do you really need to double up?

Mobile phones

A smartphone can cover most of your photography needs, but make sure you're able to back up to the cloud or your laptop, or you'll lose all your snaps if your phone goes astray. Bear in mind that phone cameras perform poorly in low light and rely on digital zooming – if you want night-time or action shots, a mobile phone may not be up to the job.

Digital cameras

DSLRs (Digital Single Lens Reflex cameras) are more versatile (and heavier) than phone cameras. Carry spare batteries and the means to charge them, and spare memory cards and a way to back them up (such as copying to your laptop or a portable hard drive). Only bring the lenses you need – consider a long zoom lens (400mm or more) for wildlife photography and a wide-angle lens for shots of interiors.

Video cameras

Video cameras are bulky and usually work best with a tripod or gimbal. Most phones can shoot video, so only bring a video camera and weighty accessories if you're sure you need them. Bear in mind that many DSLRs can record video as well as still images.

Action cameras

Compact action cameras such as the GoPro (and its many imitators) were made for capturing the giddy joy of travel. Bring a spare battery and a waterproof casing, plus any attachments you think you'll need (for example, for attaching to a motorcycle helmet).

Drones

Drones will get you amazing travel footage and annoy the heck out of anyone in the area. They're also illegal or restricted in many countries. Flying near any government, military, transport or border facility is highly risky. Unless you're a pro, leave the drone at home.

Taking a great travel photo

Tech will take you some of the way, but the art to a great travel photo is a blend of the setting, the light and your eye for photography.

Learn your tech

Don't be the traveller who buys a flashy new DSLR the week before a trip and arrives not knowing how to use it. Before you leave, read up on the functions, modes and settings, so you aren't left fumbling with the buttons while the street parade rolls out of view.

Put yourself in the situation

A long lens is handy for wildlife and distance, but for immediate, gripping travel photos, you'll need to get up close and personal with your subject matter. Bring a wide-angle lens for cramped situations, such as temple interiors and crowded marketplaces.

Be patient

Always give the picture-making process the time it deserves. When you find a good subject, look at it from different angles, try different framings – remember the 'rule of thirds' for compositions – and think about what you want from the image.

Plan your shooting time

You'll want to keep your camera handy in case something wonderful happens, but you'll usually get the best results by planning your shoots. Think about what you plan to photograph that day, the weather and light, and the best time of day to visit.

Use the light

Midday sunlight kills colours and creates shadows, bleached highlights and heavy contrast. For lively, saturated colours, use the warmer light of early morning or late afternoon. Lonely Planet's *Best Ever Photography Tips* has more advice for snappers.

Get the best image files

Bring large memory cards and shoot in RAW mode to include as much information as possible in every image file. Back up your memory cards regularly to your laptop, and then a second time to an external hard drive, so your treasured pics are protected.

MODERN-DAY MAP TIPS

Even in the digital age, maps are invaluable travel tools, even if you carry them with you on your phone. With GPS as standard, your mobile is a homing device in your pocket, so make sure you have the following apps on your phone.

Google Maps
(google.com/maps)
Whether you access it via an app or a browser, Google Maps is arguably the most useful travel tool on the net, so get it on your phone. Make full use of satellite-image mode (yes, the hotel is two blocks down the road, next to the giant tree). As well as live route-planning, you can download areas of the world to view offline, for times when you can't get a signal – Google Maps' help pages have detailed instructions.

"The mapping apps on your phone will only work if your phone is charged. Bring a (charged) power bank for emergency charging, or a quality solar charger. If you're going to the edges of the map, you might be better off with a proper handheld GPS device, such as the Garmin GPSMap (garmin.com)."

Joe Bindloss,
travel writer

Apple Maps
(apple.com/uk/maps)
Available exclusively on Apple devices, Apple Maps offers most of the features of Google Maps, in a format that's easier on the eye. It's good for route planning, but the Apple map shells show less detail than Google unless you zoom right in, and you can't take maps offline.

Citymapper
(citymapper.com)
A must for city slickers, Citymapper lets you plan your route around dozens of global hubs (New York, London, Paris, Tokyo and the like) by public transport, walking, driving and cycling, using detailed information from local transit companies.

Waze
(waze.com)
A Google subsidiary, Waze is all about satellite navigation, adding real-time crowdsourced traffic information, including reports of accidents and jams. It's great for road trips, and you can add your own alerts. Notifications of the cheapest fuel on your route can mean big savings.

All Trails
(alltrails.com)
One for outdoors enthusiasts, All Trails is a hub of user-generated trekking trails and climbing, mountain-biking and snow-sports routes. Sign up for access to trail info, photographs and route maps you can take offline, curated by fellow adventurers.

GETTING THERE & GETTING AROUND

TOP TIPS FOR FINDING FLIGHTS

Flight booking has moved on since the days of popping down to the travel agent on the high street. Today, you have the tools used by travel agents at your fingertips, but there's still an art to finding the best deal – try these tips.

MYTH BUSTING

Before we get started, there's no 'cheapest' day to book, though there are definitely cheaper days to fly. And despite what you may have heard, using your browser in 'incognito' mode or clearing cookies after every search is unlikely to make much difference to the fare.

COMPARE BOOKING SITES

Booking sites compare routes and airlines, but it's often useful to compare booking sites. Search on the comprehensive Skyscanner (skyscanner.net) or Google Flights (google.com/travel/flights) to see the prices that different travel agencies and airlines are charging for a particular route.

BOOK ONLINE

You can find almost any flight on booking sites such as Expedia (expedia.com), Momondo (momondo.com) and Kayak (kayak.com), but their algorithms may be biased towards certain carriers or routes, and sites may not show you all the fare options. It's always worth checking airline sites too, particularly for student discounts.

PAY ATTENTION TO THE ROUTE

Always sense-check the routes in the search results. Watch out for tight connections, long layovers, different outbound and return airports, and complicated combinations of airlines, which can increase the risk of missed connections and lost luggage.

"On Skyscanner, search 'everywhere' for all the options from your departure point to save money if you have no destination in mind. 'Month view' finds the cheapest day to travel. Search 'nearby airports' for both your arrival and departure to unlock all available prices."

Laura Lindsay, travel trends expert, skyscanner.net

WHEN TO BOOK

Book early. Most airlines open flights to booking about 11 months before departure. Closer to the departure date, cheaper classes fill up and availability dwindles – try to book at least five weeks ahead. Last-minute bargains are rare – prices usually increase around 21 days before departure.

UNDERSTANDING FLIGHT BOOKING

Airlines use dynamic pricing to sell seats for the highest price they can get, so fares go up and down with demand. Seats are released in staggered batches, with smaller allocations in the cheaper brackets – if you see a good price, grab it.

SHOP THE SALES

Many airlines offer sales in January, September and dates such as Black Friday. Sign up for airline newsletters and travel news services such as going.com and theflightdeal.com for prior notice. Always investigate whether the price really offers a saving.

BEWARE SEASONAL PRICE HIKES

Everyone wants to fly at the weekend, or during the school holidays, or when the weather is best for sunbathing. If you fly outside of these peak times, there'll be more seats at lower prices. Compare prices between Christmas and New Year to those two weeks before and after to see what we mean!

BE A MIDWEEK FLIER

Demand and prices peak at weekends, while Tuesday and Wednesday are usually the cheapest days to fly. Click on the date field while searching on Google Flights to bring up a calendar showing how prices vary on different dates. Most airline websites display a calendar of daily fares when you search, making it easy to spot the cheap days to fly.

UNDERSTANDING BUDGET AIRLINES

Budget carriers don't always come up in booking-site searches, and fares can be gratifyingly inexpensive if you book early, but be wary of hidden charges and taxes. Unless you can fit everything into a single carry-on bag, you'll have to pay extra for a hold bag. Meals and drinks are extra too, and there may be penalty charges if you don't check in online within a specified time frame. As you go through the booking process, watch for automatically selected, paid-for 'extras' – such as seat selection, travel insurance or priority boarding – and be ready to deselect anything you don't want to pay for.

PLOT YOUR ROUTE

Your destination might be an island with only one airport, but that might not be the best way to get there. There could be a larger, busier airport nearby, just a short ferry-ride away. Try these tips for route planning.

★ Find out who flies where

As a first step, investigate which airlines fly to your destination. Wikipedia pages for specific airports usually include a list of airlines and destinations that you can use as a rough starting point. Continue the search for direct routes on airline websites and at FlightConnections (flightconnections.com) and FlightMapper (flightmapper.net).

★ Direct or connect?

Flying to your destination without stopping is the quickest choice, but it might not be the cheapest. Competition between airlines is fierce, so look out for cheaper fares combining a short-haul flight to a nearby country and then a long-haul flight from their main hub.

★ Multiple airlines?

Be wary about booking connecting flights with different airlines. If the whole route is covered by a single airline, they're responsible for getting you and your bags to your destination if you miss your connection. If multiple carriers are involved, you might be on your own if the first flight is delayed.

★ Layover tips

For any connecting flight, check the layover time. Less than two hours might be too tight to make your connection; more than four hours means a long, boring wait. Allow extra time if changing airlines;

always check if flights leave from the same terminal and see if you need to collect your bags and check in for the second flight.

★ Fly nearby

Check out alternative airports close to where you want to go – eg Charleroi and Beauvais for Paris; or Stansted, Luton and Southend for London. Clicking on the map in a Google Flights search will reveal prices for flights to all the airports in the vicinity. Budget airlines fly to hundreds of smaller airports, but always factor in the price of local transport to your final destination.

Make your flights count

When it comes to aviation, points mean prizes, so make full use of loyalty programmes, credit cards and frequent-flier programmes.

Be a frequent flier

Always join the frequent-flier programme – or claim the points if you're part of an affiliated scheme. Members of the big airline alliances (SkyTeam, Star Alliance and Oneworld) offer reciprocal credits for frequent fliers of partner airlines. Some hotel loyalty schemes will also let you claim credits for qualifying stays in the form of points for partner airlines.

Credit & loyalty cards

Credit cards linked to Air Miles, Avios or airline point schemes are a great way to build up credits. Use your credit card widely (and promptly settle the balance each month) and your points tally will soar. Don't overlook click-through points on shopping and dining portals run by airlines such as British Airways (shopping.ba.com) and Virgin Atlantic (shopsaway. virginatlantic.com), and supermarket loyalty cards such as Nectar and Tesco's Clubcard.

"The most obvious ways to get airline frequent-flier miles are through flying or credit cards. But there are many other ways, including buying everyday items online through the airline's shopping portal, linking your credit cards to airline dining programmes, crediting car rentals to the airline loyalty programme or even taking online surveys."

Scott Mayerowitz,
head of editorial, The Points Guy
(thepointsguy.com)

Use your points

Airlines set aside an allocation of seats for award bookings, so you can't use your points for every flight, and you'll have to pay the tax, fuel surcharges and airport service charges, even if the ticket is free. However, the points threshold for booking business-class and first-class seats might be lower than you think. Search for 'award' or 'reward' flights on airline websites and remember that award points can be used for upgrades as well as new bookings.

GETTING AN UPGRADE

Don't expect to be bumped up to first class just for smiling sweetly. Airlines give priority to frequent-flyer club members with healthy points balances or people with special reasons for upgrading – for example, a broken leg. Dressing smartly, asking politely and arriving early will increase your chances. If the airline asks for volunteers to be bumped onto a later flight, see if you can get an upgrade as part of the deal. Upgrades are a solo traveller's game – nobody gets an upgrade for the whole family.

HOW TO ARRIVE REFRESHED

You've seen those frequent fliers who roll off a long-haul flight looking fresh as a spring morning, while you look like a straggler at a music festival. Try these tips for keeping yourself well in the air.

Stay hydrated

Cabin air is notoriously dry, and drinking alcohol and drinks containing caffeine will dehydrate you even further. Savvy travellers stick to juice and water. Your skin isn't immune – use moisturiser, and saline eye drops if you're prone to dry eyes.

Keep moving

Periodically walk around the cabin to keep your blood flowing freely, reducing the risk of deep vein thrombosis (DVT). Raising and lowering your feet while sitting will also help with blood flow.

Avoid motion sickness

If you're prone to travel sickness, get a window seat between or forward of the wings, for maximum stability. Don't eat salty, oily or spicy foods, avoid reading or using screens, turn on the overhead air vents, and carry Dramamine (or ginger) as a fallback option.

Rest

Although it may be tempting to binge-watch all five seasons of *Breaking Bad*, sleeping is probably a better use of your flight time. A travel pillow and an eye mask can help – sitting at a window seat can bring more control over light levels and less chance of being disturbed.

Dress to fly

No, we don't mean a flying jacket and leather goggles. Plane cabins get colder after hours at high altitude, so wear layers you can remove and put back on as needed, and bring a scarf or a shawl as an extra layer.

If you can, lie down

If you have spare seats next to you, raise your legs to the same level as your head for better sleep. To maximise the chances of an empty row, choose a seat in the back few rows (but not the very last row).

© UNDREY / SHUTTERSTOCK

Maximise legroom

If you're tall (or just like space), book a seat by the emergency exits or bulkheads for more legroom. To keep your seat, say you're OK helping with emergency procedures. For bulkhead seats, bring earplugs – you'll be sharing with babies in travel cots.

Pick a seat for easy boarding

Larger modern airports use jet bridges attached to the front of the aircraft, so book seats towards the front for quick boarding and disembarking. If planes use movable steps, you'll just have to take your chances.

Check in early

To minimise stress, check in at least three hours ahead for international flights, or two hours for domestic routes. Go to the gate in plenty of time – you don't want to be halfway across the terminal when they announce, 'Last call for Flight 57.'

Scope out your journey

Do some research into the airports that you're arriving at and departing from – and the aircraft you'll be flying on. Use SeatGuru (seatguru.com) and the Flio (flio.com) and LoungeBuddy (loungebuddy.com) apps to scope out flights and seats, as well as airport layouts and lounges.

Prep for security

Keep your liquids ready in a clear plastic bag, and another bag handy for your wallet, phone and watch when you go through security. Remove your belt and take out your laptop before you reach the scanners.

Be disembarking-ready

When the pilot makes the 'we will shortly be descending' announcement, put things back into your bags, check the seat pocket, pop your shoes back on, and sit back in Zen-like calm while other passengers scrabble for their belongings on landing.

Beat jetlag

Jetlag is always worse going east, so rest as much as possible on the flight and immediately adjust your sleep schedule to the local time. If you arrive by day, only go to bed at the local bedtime (taking melatonin may help). If you arrive by night, set an early alarm and go out into the daylight to reset your circadian rhythms.

Going round-the-world

There's a lot of mileage in a round-the-world ticket from one of the big airline alliances. Try these hacks to get the best from your circumnavigation.

Routes

Round-the-world makes it sound like anything is possible, but tickets usually target a small collection of hub cities, and you can only fly with airlines that are part of the alliance, so pick stops according to your interests and budget. Tickets visiting Africa and South America tend to cost more – stick to Europe–Asia–Australia–America for the lowest fares.

Understand the terms

For most tickets, you must keep going in one direction, heading either east or west (the latter is better for avoiding jetlag) and finishing where you started. Most tickets allow for six to nine stops over the space of 12 months, but avoid backtracking as the price is based on the total mileage.

Tack on a detour

You don't have to stick to just the destinations on your round-the-world ticket. Book cheap seats on budget airlines to add interesting detours to neighbouring countries, such as side-trips to Cambodia, Vietnam or Indonesia from Bangkok, Singapore or Kuala Lumpur.

When to go round-the-world

There are good times to go round-the-world. Heading east, start your trip between mid-April and June, and you'll follow good weather around the planet, catching one summer in Australia and one summer in the US. This also coincides with the best prices for round-the-world tickets.

Squeeze in some overlanding

Better round-the-world tickets include some open-jaw segments, allowing you to cross larger countries overland, before flying out again on the far side. Look for tickets with exciting open sections in Australia, Asia and the US.

© WEERAKARN SATTNIRAMAI / GETTY IMAGES; JO0830908 / SHUTTERSTOCK

GETTING OUT OF THE AIRPORT

Grabbing a bargain flight is only half the equation. Getting from terminal to town is another situation where you can be fleeced or find a bargain – here's how smart travellers do it.

★ Split the cost

The cost of a taxi to town will drop significantly if you share it with other passengers, so ask around at the baggage carousel (you'll have better luck with solo travellers and couples).

★ Airport taxis

Be wary of pricey private companies trying to attract your attention in the arrivals hall and look instead for the official, regulated airport taxi (or autorickshaw) service. You may need to pay in advance, but the fare will be fixed, and usually lower than haggling with the drivers in front of the terminal.

★ Rideshares

Drivers for Uber, Lyft and other rideshare companies are often prohibited from picking up and dropping off at the terminal, but they can usually stop within walking distance, and fares are usually lower than airport taxis.

★ Local buses

Many airports run a dedicated low-cost airport bus or minivan service to town. For an even cheaper ride, see if any local bus routes pass in front of the airport – the journey may take longer, and you'll usually need to pop your luggage on your lap, but the fare will be tiny.

★ Mass transit

The world's best airports are integrated into city mass transit systems, meaning easy, inexpensive transfers to town by train. See if you can save money by buying a transport pass instead of a single or return ticket.

★ Hire cars

Picking up a car at the airport is certainly convenient, but you'll pay more than if you hire downtown. Check if any 'flight + car hire' deals are available when you book, and make sure you're aware of the parking rules in town and have the means to pay for any toll roads.

Why fly?

Do you really need to fly? Scope out alternative ways to travel on Rome2Rio (rometorio.com) – the planet will thank you. Here are more hacks for a greener, leaner trip.

"Make the most of joined-up transport links by travelling by train then ferry to reach islands in the Mediterranean, such as the Balearics, Corsica, Sardinia and Sicily. Rail bookings are often released just a few months before travel, so sign up to free email alert services offered by rail agencies, such as raileurope.com, which let you know as soon as bookings open."

Richard Hammond,
founder of
greentraveller.co.uk

Let the train take the strain

Trains offer some big advantages over flying, beyond the carbon saving. Stations are usually central, check-in procedures are streamlined, you can move around easily, and your bags are on hand throughout the journey. Plus, train fares are usually cheaper than airfares, particularly after you factor in airport transfers.

Go by boat

Taking the boat will cut your emissions, and you'll have the luxury of space to stroll about and restaurants where you can order from a proper menu. Useful international boat routes include cross-Channel services from the UK to Europe, car ferries from Europe to North Africa and inter-island ferries in Southeast Asia, the Mediterranean and the Caribbean. Visit www.travellerspoint.com/guide/International_ferries/ to investigate the options.

Take the car

Car insurers will cover you to drive in neighbouring countries for a small surcharge, often with local breakdown support included. Keep all the vehicle paperwork handy and read up on the local road rules. If there's water in the way, find the nearest roll-on, roll-off (RORO) ferry, or pop your car on the Eurotunnel train (eurotunnel.com) linking the UK and Europe.

Tips for international drivers

Always check if your home driving licence is valid in your chosen destination. If not, grab an International Driving Permit (IDP; internationaldrivingpermit.org). Investigate the vehicle rules for local drivers – you might need specific items of emergency equipment or stickers to deflect the glare from your headlights – and contact local driving organisations such as the American Automobile Association (aaa.com) for detailed tips.

On your bike

With a pedal cycle, you can cut your emissions even further. If you're a paying foot passenger, you can take your bike for free on many trains and boats, and most airlines will carry properly packed bikes for a surcharge (for tips, see cyclinguk.org/cyclists-library/bikes-public-transport/bikes-air).

GET A PASS

Transport is going to eat up a big chunk of your travel budget, but travel passes offer bargains if you know how to use them. Read on...

Interrail & Eurail

Long-distance travel in Europe is a breeze with the Interrail Pass (interrail.eu) for European citizens, which covers unlimited train travel in 33 countries for a set number of days within a fixed period (priced from €194–€711). Work out routes using the Interrail Rail Planner app. For non-EU-residents, the Eurail Pass (eurail.com) offers a similar deal. Under-27s get discounts of up to 25%.

Other rail passes

Rail passes are rare in Asia, Africa and South America, but the United States's Amtrak (amtrak.com) and Canada's Via Rail (viarail.ca) have schemes that offer modest savings. The price of the Amtrak USA Rail Pass is good for 10 segments over 30 days – the price drops from US$499 to US$299 during Amtrak's regular sales. Don't overlook rail discount cards within individual countries – see p52.

Unlimited passes for bus travel

There are a few useful bus-pass schemes in big countries with big cross-country bus companies. Greyhound Australia's Whimit Pass (greyhound.com.au/travel-passes) offers unlimited bus travel for 120 days for A$369, while New Zealand's Intercity offers the Flexipass (intercity.co.nz/bus-pass), which is good for 10 to 80 hours of bus travel (priced from NZ$139 to NZ$641).

Top air passes

Major airline networks offer a handful of passes where you can book coupons for a fixed number of trips within a particular region (Australia, Asia, Africa) in conjunction with an inbound international ticket, but savings are modest. The single-continent Visit Passes from Oneworld (oneworld.com) are probably the most useful. Contact the networks by phone for details. Round-the-world tickets (see p44) may be more useful if you have a particular route in mind.

Trips with added value

Travelling involves plenty of, well, travel, so you want to make the most of the experience. Here are some great ways to make your journey count.

Travel overnight

Travel on an overnight flight, boat, bus or train and you'll save the cost of a night's accommodation and cover big distances without eating into your sightseeing time. On overnight ferries, sleeping in your seat or on deck offers savings compared with booking a berth. If you go by sleeper train, look for shared compartments with open sets of bunks, which cost less and offer opportunities to mingle with other passengers. For overnight bus rides, seek out 'Luxury', '2 by 2' or 'Superdeluxe' buses with reclining seats.

Take scenic routes by day

If the journey is particularly scenic – rolling through the Rocky Mountains by train, for example, or flying alongside Himalayan peaks in Nepal – aim to travel by day. Find out in advance which side of the vehicle offers the best views and book a seat early by the window. In the developing world, the best views from trains are often from the open doorways between the carriages; when travelling by boat, stake out a spot with a view up on deck.

© RICHARD JACYNO / GETTY IMAGES

Take the interesting route

Zipping straight from A to B might save time, but you'll miss out on all the interesting stops along the way. Whenever you plan a route, zoom in on the map to see if there are any interesting detours along the way (using Google Maps in 'satellite' view is great for spotting intriguing geological features and off-the-beaten-track sights).

Offset the carbon

Keeping carbon emissions down is a priority, but you're bound to emit some CO_2 on your trip. Consider contributing to an ethical carbon-offsetting scheme that invests in active carbon-reduction measures. Seek out projects with Gold Standard verification (goldstandard.org) and visit ethicalconsumer.org for more tips.

MAKE THE JOURNEY THE DESTINATION

It isn't all about getting to the end of the line – on plenty of trips, the journey is the star. Travelling overland promises sights, experiences and cultural encounters that you'd never experience in an aluminium tube in the sky. Here are our favourite overland epics.

The Reunification Express

What's the best way to see a long, thin country like Vietnam? On a long, thin train of course! The Reunification Express started service at the end of the Vietnam War, linking former enemies Hanoi and Ho Chi Minh City in just over 31 hours, with swoon-inducing views of jungles, rice paddies and the South China Sea along the way.

Across India by train

Indian Railways (indianrail.gov. in) links every corner of this vast nation, via 68,103km (42,317 miles) of tracks. Travelling in Sleeper Class, First Class or in two-tier AC and three-tier AC carriages, you can travel from the foothills of the Himalaya to the beaches of the steamy south with a tiny carbon footprint, enjoying intense cultural immersion for every rattling mile.

Island-hopping through Greece

Buzzing around the Greek islands by boat and bike feels like embarking on your own mini odyssey, tracing shipping routes made legendary by Homer, Hesiod and Sophocles. Arrive by air or rail into Athens and the ports of Piraeus, Rafina and Lavrio offer easy access to dozens of islands, from well-trodden Crete and Santorini to low-key isles such as Lemnos.

By bus through Central America

Easy border-crossings make for epic bus journeys through Central America. Start in Mexico and zigzag to beaches, volcanoes and lost cities in Guatemala, Belize, El Salvador, Honduras, Nicaragua, Costa Rica and Panama, where boats take you around the Darién Gap to South America.

Overland through Patagonia

A hire car or local buses can transport you through some of the most humbling landscapes on Earth as you cross between Chile and Argentina. Continue up the drier west coast of the continent for easy access to Bolivia, Peru, Ecuador and Colombia.

"Sometimes it's the journey that lingers longest in the memory. I'll never forget the motorcycle ride from Ladakh to Kashmir in India. Infrastructure was threadbare, the roads were ragged and I had to deal with sunburn, chapped lips and intense cold, but the sense of freedom and liberation was unparalleled."

Joe Bindloss, travel writer

Overlanding hacks

Plenty of agencies offer overland adventures, but it's cheaper and more liberating to make your own arrangements – try these top tips.

"The best overland vehicle you can own is the one you already have. Concentrate on the vehicle's reliability and simplicity so that you can focus on your journey. Building yourself an overlander? Avoid base vehicle modifications and keep it as stock as possible. It will be easier and cheaper to fix no matter where in the world the road takes you."

Angela Devaney, co-founder, Mowgli Adventures (mowgli-adventures.com)

ROUTES ACROSS THE WORLD

For Europeans, ferry routes to Morocco, Tunisia and Algeria open up a second continent worthy of road trips, including the epic Trans-African Highway from Cairo to Cape Town. North America was the birthplace of road-tripping and the land border with Mexico promises easy overlanding as far as Panama. Even bigger adventures await beyond the Darién Gap in South America. Grab a copy of the *Overlanders' Handbook* by Chris Scott or visit overlandtrailguides.com and roadtrippers.com for more inspiration.

THE RIGHT OVERLAND VEHICLE

Almost any vehicle can be made into an overlanding machine, but you'll need a 4WD for off-road driving. Pick a vehicle with an old-fashioned, low-tech engine – Land Rover Defenders and Toyota Land Cruisers are favourites. Carry spare fuel, food and water, a spare tyre and air compressor, and a mobile phone so you can call for help, plus a full emergency repair kit. Adding a toilet and shower is advanced level – you're better off buying an off-the-shelf recreational vehicle. The blogs mowgli-adventures.com and takethetruck. com are packed with vehicle tips.

CROSS-BORDER DRIVING

Taking hire cars across borders can be tricky – it's better to bring your own vehicle and get a Carnet de Passage; contact Alliance Internationale de Tourisme (ait-touringalliance.com) or Federation Internationale de l'Automobile (fia.com) for info. Ensure your home insurance covers the trip (or buy a local top-up) and check the requirements for each border crossing.

GEAR FOR THE ROAD

Use stacking plastic tubs to keep things organised and lash them down with straps or bungee cords to stop them flying about. If you don't have a fridge, use a cold-box and shop-bought ice or frozen plastic bottles of water. If you don't have an in-vehicle cooker, bring a portable stove (ideally powered by gasoline rather than butane cannisters).

Self-drive for less

Car hire prices vary wildly, but a few things are constant. Here's how to hire for less.

Quick hire hacks

Book early for the widest choice of companies and vehicles, and make sure the car is big enough for your needs – some 'compact' cars will barely accommodate a handbag. Local companies usually charge less than Hertz, Avis and friends – look out for 'flight+car' deals on travel booking sites. See if you can pick up in town rather than at the airport for lower rates.

Common hire pitfalls

Take a photo with your mobile phone to record any existing scratches and dents when you pick up to avoid disputes later. Renting with unlimited mileage is normally safer than trying to predict your driving patterns – before you return the vehicle, fill up the tank to avoid expensive refuelling charges, and use a petrol station vacuum cleaner to remove all that beach sand!

One-way hires

In big-scale destinations such as the US, Canada and Australia, look for companies specialising in 'relocation' – moving vehicles around the country for car-hire firms and people moving home – such as Imoova (imoova.com) and Transfercar (transfercarus.com).

Licences & age limits

Few hire companies will rent to under-21s (under-23s in some countries), and some vehicle classes are off-limits to the under-25s. Check the driving licence rules – if you need an International Driving Permit, apply before you travel.

Insurance

At the very minimum, you need insurance for the vehicle, along with any vehicles and people you might be unlucky enough to collide with. Consider paying more for a Collision Damage Waiver (CDW) to drop the excess – rates may be lower through third-party insurers, such as reducemyexcess.co.uk. Check whether your credit card includes insurance cover as standard.

Hiring a car & driver

Costs for hiring a car with a driver can be very reasonable if shared with a few fellow travellers. Normally, you'll be responsible for fuel and your own eating and sleeping requirements, while the driver makes their own arrangements.

"Writing off a jeep in a national park in Kenya was a painful lesson in always reading the small print on hire-car insurance policies. The Collision Damage Waiver covered the vehicle, but not the windscreen or the (undamaged) tyres, which I had to pay for."

Joe Bindloss,
travel writer

THE TRAVEL HACK HANDBOOK

HACK THE RAILS

"Sleeper trains let you cover long distances time-effectively while you save on a hotel bill. In Europe or Asia, book a berth – sitting up in a standard seat is a false economy. But in the US and Canada, where seats are spacious with a good recline, they're comfy enough for overnight trips."

Mark Smith, the Man in Seat 61 (seat61.com)

You don't have to be a trainspotter to love travelling by rail. There's often a view, you can stretch your legs and it's easy to chat to locals. Here are our top train tips.

GET A RAILCARD

If you don't have a rail pass (see p47) look into getting a local rail discount card, such as the UK's Britrail Pass (britrail.com) or Railcard (railcard.co.uk), or France's SNCF Avantage card (sncf.com). For an annual fee, you'll get discounts every time you travel. There are cards for families, young people and older travellers – to find out what's available, check in with the local rail companies.

BE AN EARLY BIRD

Train tickets get increasingly expensive the closer you get to the day of travel, peaking for same-day travel. Tickets are normally released about 12 weeks before departure – try to book at least a week before you travel to avoid peak fares. Look at the time of travel too; prices fall outside of the peak weekday commuting hours (usually 6.30am to 9.30am and 4pm to 7pm).

MAKE THE MILES COUNT

You'll see much more from a train than from a plane or bus, so always take the train (and sit by the window) for daytime journeys through scenic country. Trains also make for easy stopovers, as you can book your onward train before you leave the station – check ahead to see if there's a left-luggage office so you can buzz around the sights for a few hours unencumbered.

© MICHAEL HEFFERNAN / LONELY PLANET

CHECK IN WITH THE CONDUCTOR

In many countries, the train conductor or stationmaster can help you overcome all manner of obstacles, from finding a seat on a train you've already boarded to working out alternative ways to get to your destination if you miss the train. If you get into trouble, find these useful characters and see what they can do.

TAKE THE SLEEPER

For long journeys, book a sleeper berth and save on hotels. First-class usually means air-con, a meal service and extra comfort; cheaper compartments have more berths, but it's easier to meet fellow passengers. Upper berths offer more privacy and you may be able to leave your berth folded out for daytime dozes.

RESERVATION HACKS

Unreserved seating can be cheap, but you might end up sitting on your bag in the aisle. If you have the option to reserve a seat, do it. Book early to secure a coveted seat with a table or a window seat on a scenic ride. Think about which way you'll be facing – away from the direction of travel can aggravate motion sickness.

PLAN YOUR ROUTE

Before you take the train, get to know the network. Try the website of the national rail company, or look for a national rail website, such as the UK's National Rail (nationalrail.co.uk). Alternatively, try booking sites like thetrainline.com, raileurope.com and 12go.asia, or the Eurail/Interrail Rail Planner app. For country-by-country guides, there's no better site than seat61.com.

CATCH THAT TRAIN

Nobody wants to chase a moving train down the platform. Some stations are maze-like warrens, and some trains are longer than city blocks, so get to the station early. Give yourself an hour before departure to locate your platform (or find someone to ask if there are no departure boards or announcements); you'll also have time to grab drinks and snacks – and a newspaper, magazine or novel if you still have time to kill.

Ride the waves

Travelling by boat means approaching your destination like a 19th-century seafarer arriving in an uncharted land – it's vastly more romantic than descending into yet another faceless airport. Try these hacks to find your sea legs.

Check the timetables

Don't rely on being able to travel just because there's a ferry route marked on the map. Some routes stop running when the seas are rough, or when rivers become swollen during the rains or are too shallow during the dry season. For ferry route info and bookings, try websites such as 12go.asia, directferries.co.uk and ferryhopper.com.

Missed the ferry?

If the journey is an hour or less, small boat operators may be willing to whisk you across for a fee, though it will be much more expensive than the usual ferry fare. Check if there are any other ferry companies running from other jetties in the area – if you go island-hopping from Athens, there are departures from Piraeus, Rafina and Lavrio, all within 40km (25 miles) of the capital.

Self-skipper

Bareboat charter agencies such as Sunsail (sunsail.co.uk) and websites such as Click&Boat (clickandboat.com) can get you out on the water with minimum fuss if you have an International Certificate of Competence (ICC) and Day Skipper qualification. If not, charter a boat with a skipper, or stick to somewhere used to renting boats to beginners, such as Australia's Whitsunday Islands or the Aegean. Don't overlook canals and other inland waterways – you rarely need previous experience to hire a dayboat on freshwater.

Safety on the water

Life jackets are often in short supply and emergency escape routes may be blocked, so park yourself up on deck or close to the exit. Make sure you can swim confidently, and avoid small boats, which are more prone to getting into difficulties. Never board an overcrowded ferry – if there are more passengers than seats, find another boat. Check the weather too; if there's a storm approaching, sit it out on land.

TWO WHEELS GOOD

Going by bike is as green as it gets, and you can start pedalling right from your front door. However, it takes a bit of planning, as you'll need cyclable roads and transport that lets you carry your wheels. These tips will get you rolling.

"Before you go, try at least one day's riding with your entire touring setup, especially bags and clothing. This is the best – and only – way to work out what might rub, what's about to fall off and how your body will stand up to what you're about to do."

Tom Hall, avid cyclist and vice-president, Lonely Planet

Transport your bike for free

You can often carry your bike for free (or for a nominal charge) as a foot passenger on a train or boat. Find out in advance if you can travel with your bike assembled, or if you need to pack it in a bike bag or box. Some trains, including French TGV services, only accept packed bikes. Reservations are often mandatory for bikes on busy commuter trains, so get in early, or travel off-peak.

Pack your bike for flying

Contact your airline to see exactly how they require bikes to be packed, and the charges and weight limit. You'll usually need a bike bag or box, and you'll need to remove the pedals, turn the handlebars in line with the front wheel, and deflate the tyres. Airlines prefer the packed bike to measure less than 1m (3ft) across (ideally less than 85cm/2.8ft). Removing the front wheel and lowering the seat (or removing the seat post) will help. Install a dummy axle to stop the forks being accidentally crushed.

Rent on arrival

Hiring a bike when you get there may be easier. Rental bikes are easy to find in tourist hubs, but you'll generally have to return the bike to where you picked it up, and it's harder to find touring bikes with panniers. Don't overlook city-based bikeshare schemes for local exploring.

Supported cycling trips

Supported cycle touring holidays are easy to arrange almost everywhere – including adventurous destinations such as India and Morocco through operators such as exodus.co.uk and explore.co.uk. Just search online for 'cycle touring' and your chosen destination.

Go forth on foot

Walking will cut your carbon footprint dramatically and you'll get a free workout every day of the trip. Here are our top hiking hacks.

1 Check your route
Always investigate the route before you set off by talking to locals or consulting trail guidebooks or All Trails (alltrails.com) – go with a guide if you don't know the terrain. Carry a GPS (and a map and compass as backup), and bring a phone and power-bank charger so you can call for help in an emergency.

2 Check the weather
Bad weather can make trekking dangerous, as well as miserable. Use a weather app such as Accuweather (accuweather.com) as your eye on the skies; if the weather deteriorates, pause somewhere safe rather than pushing on to your next overnight stop.

3 Be a lightweight
Every gram counts when you're the packhorse; if you don't need it, leave it at home. Carry a smaller pack – under 65L – so you aren't tempted to cram in every hiking gadget under the sun.

4 Let there be light
You never know when you might need to find your way in the dark, so bring a lightweight LED torch or headlamp. Carry spare batteries (and keep them dry).

5 Keep it dry
Backpack covers may keep your stuff dry – a heavy-duty binbag inside your pack definitely will. Use smaller press-seal or ziplock bags to protect items such as maps, matches and electronics.

6 Keep yourself dry
A quality waterproof jacket is another must – if only for your own morale! Bring some foldback stationery clips and a length of nylon string as an impromptu washing line in case you get wet.

7 Purify your own water
Avoid buying water in plastic bottles – carry a refillable bottle or canteen and use a water purifier pump (with a filter of less than 0.2 microns) or water treatment drops or tablets based on chlorine dioxide. In an emergency, boil water for at least a minute (or more at high elevations).

8 Break in your boots
Shiny new boots mean blisters – unless, of course, you break them in first. Always take some practice hikes at home before putting your new footwear to the test on the trails.

9 Don't go hungry
Carry some high-carb, nutrient-rich foodstuffs for an emergency energy boost. Nuts, dried fruit, protein bars and instant mashed potatoes are tried and tested.

© KAMILA STARZYCKA / SHUTTERSTOCK; PRZEMEK KLOS / SHUTTERSTOCK

Top tip

"I always go with an older guide – they have less to prove and are generally more dependable – but solo women trekkers might be more comfortable with a female trekking guide. Try to sit down with any prospective guide beforehand and go through the proposed route on a map. It will quickly be apparent whether they really know the area."

Bradley Mayhew, author of Lonely Planet's Trekking in the Nepal Himalaya

10 Stay warm

Use layers to manage your body temperature, and make sure at least one of them is windproof. On cold nights, fill your water bottle with hot water and stuff it into a sock as an improvised water bottle (you can drink it in the morning).

11 Don't be a mosquito magnet

Use an insect repellent with a high concentration of diethyltoluamide (DEET) and a quality mosquito net or coils when you sleep. Avoid dark clothing – it attracts the little blighters.

12 Check your body for ticks & leeches

Always conduct a thorough body scan before you get into bed for the night, and remove any bloodsuckers carefully, then disinfect the wound. See p130 for more advice on health matters.

13 Charge your devices

You need to be able to charge your phone, so carry a charged power bank or a solar-powered charger. Find models with direct charging (at least 28W) from makers like BigBlue (bigblue-tech.com).

14 Tell someone where you're going

Wise trekkers never walk alone. Go with at least one companion, and always tell someone where you are going and when you expect to be back – whether that's the hotel where you're leaving your non-trekking luggage, your embassy, or people back home.

15 Leave no trace

Responsible trekkers never leave a trace of their trek on the trails. Bring a plastic bag to transport any rubbish back down the trail with you, and bury any toilet waste well away from water sources.

Urban transport for pros

Getting around a big city can be expensive – or cheap as chips if you know the local transport hacks.

 ## FREE URBAN TRANSPORT

Some destinations offer free transport on city buses or trams, including such hubs as Tallinn, Perth (Australia) and Kansas City – and the whole of Malta and Luxembourg (find more destinations at freepublictransport.info). If you're a young person or senior citizen, keep your ID handy as there may be discounts – all buses, trams, trains and boats in Budapest, for example, are free for EU citizens aged 65 or over.

 ## GET A TRANSPORT PASS

Use smart passes that work across the entire public transport network, rather than buying individual tickets. Usually you'll get a discount on the single-ride fare, and the card becomes valid for unlimited transport that day once you hit a fare threshold. Always check how the system works – with London's Oyster scheme (oyster.tfl.gov.uk), you can tap with a contactless bank card and get the same benefits – and confirm if you need to scan in and out on each journey to avoid fines.

 ## SHARE THE RIDE

Rather than paying peak rates for a licensed city cab, summon a rideshare from Uber (uber.com), Lyft (lyft.com) or the local rideshare company and you'll (usually) pay less and have a record of your trip, vehicle and driver for added peace of mind. Ask around to see which apps locals are using – Uber doesn't operate everywhere. Don't overlook carpooling apps, such as BlaBlaCar (blablacar.com), for another cheap way to ride.

 ## POWER BY PEDAL

Bikeshare schemes cover everything from pedal cycles to electric bikes and e-scooters, and they're great for urban exploring. Be careful in traffic as the bikes tend to be fairly clunky. For longer rides, consider renting a 'proper' bike with a helmet from a local bike shop. Investigate how each scheme works before you sign up – some bikes can be parked anywhere, others need to be returned to designated docks, which may not cover every part of town.

TRAVEL FOR FREE (YOU HEARD US)

Believe it or not, there is such a thing as a free lunch (and even a free flight, hotel and dinner). Plenty of people get paid to travel – here's how to be one of them.

"With a CELTA teaching qualification, you can find work all over the world, giving private tuition. Private language schools typically follow the regular school calendar, so try to time your applications to coincide with the start of the academic year. Demand for English-speakers has never been greater – where I live in Italy, schools are crying out for qualified mother-tongue teachers in the wake of post-Brexit shortfalls."

Duncan Garwood, travel writer and English language teacher (@ DuncanGarwood)

Work in travel

Holiday companies need staff every season, and plenty of jobs come with free (or discounted) accommodation and sometimes even cut-price flights. For repping work at resorts, contact big package holiday companies such as Tui (careers.tuigroup.com/holiday-destination-jobs). For ski teaching and chalet work, try big winter resorts such as Vail (jobs.vailresortscareers.com) or ski sites such as Skiworld (skiworld.co.uk). For many sport-teaching jobs, you'll need relevant qualifications – some dive and ski schools will subsidise your training if you commit to working for them for a season.

Be a roaming reporter

Every travel article and travel book you've ever seen (including this one) was written by someone who was paid to travel by newspapers, magazines, websites and book publishers. You can add in bloggers and

influencers, though it takes a special combination of dedication, hard work and luck to be successful in either arena. Get your foot in the door by pitching travel pieces about your home country to local travel editors and build from there.

Work remotely

Working for a company in another country means lots of red tape, but there's nothing stopping you working for your usual clients from somewhere else. Thousands of digital nomads make a full-time lifestyle out of travelling and working remotely in IT, publishing, even accounting – setting up

temporary bases in nomad hubs such as Bali, Lisbon and Buenos Aires. Check out Lonely Planet's *Digital Nomad Handbook* for detailed tips and advice.

Teach a language

Language teaching has transported untold thousands of travellers around the globe, and many teaching programmes include a salary and free room and board, particularly in Japan and South Korea. Start by getting a teaching qualification – TEFL and TESOL are the most widely recognised schemes for English speakers. Explore the process at tefl.org and tefl.com.

SEE THE SIGHTS FOR LESS

TEN TOP FREE THINGS TO SEE

"Some of my favourite travel experiences cost nothing at all. In Asia, I like to get up at first light to visit temples, monasteries and mosques. There's rarely a charge to enter, and by visiting early, you can experience these sacred sites as locals do, before the crowds arrive."

Joe Bindloss, travel writer

Seeing the sights is what travel is all about, but include too many and you might have to go home early due to bankruptcy. Our favourites offer maximum wonder for minimum outlay.

1 The Kensington Museums, London

A triptych of museums – the Natural History Museum, the Victoria & Albert Museum and the Science Museum – offer a staggering dose of culture for free.

2 St Peter's Basilica, Rome

There's no charge to visit the most famous church in the world, with its supersized dome, celestial interior and colonnaded piazza.

3 The Staten Island Ferry, New York

New York City's legendary free ferry service doubles as a tour of one of the world's most famous harbours, with front-row views of the Statue of Liberty.

4 Thiksey Gompa, Ladakh

Famed for its butter sculptures, sand mandalas and murals, this medieval monastery has been filling the high Himalaya with mantras for a thousand years.

5 798 Art District, Běijīng

This one-time industrial quarter, reinvented as China's leading hub for modern art, is home to buzzing galleries and the free Ullens Center for Contemporary Art (UCCA).

6 Royal Botanic Gardens Victoria, Melbourne

Australia's best botanic garden has possums, cockatoos and kookaburras, and rare beasts like the southern brown bandicoot.

7 The Blue Mosque, İstanbul

While you'll have to plan a visit around prayer times, there's no charge to explore this stunning set of minarets and domes.

8 Sensō-ji, Tokyo

Approach Tokyo's most revered temple on foot through the heaving Nakamise-dōri market, passing pilgrims, geishas, tourists and stalls full of Japanese treats.

9 The Medina, Fez

Get lost in this maze of blind turns and winding alleys – one of the oldest and largest marketplaces in the world – to find the mercantile soul of Morocco.

10 Trekking around El Chaltén, Argentina

There's no fee to hike into the epic Patagonian landscapes of Los Glaciares National Park from this legendary trekking hub.

Five top travel swaps

Put off by the price of a trip to the Grand Canyon? Balking at the queue to the Louvre? Fear not, there are always alternatives; try these top switcheroos.

★ Swap the Grand Canyon for Canyon de Chelly National Monument

Nothing can compete with the Grand Canyon for sheer drama, but visiting can burn a canyon-sized hole in your bank account. For giant-sized landscapes without the financial sting, head to nearby Canyon de Chelly National Monument (nps.gov/cach) – entry is free, landscapes are epic and you can explore Ancestral Puebloan dwellings with Navajo guides.

★ Swap the Louvre for the Petit Palais

Great art comes with a hefty price tag at Paris's most famous art museum, but there's free art on the same stretch of the Seine at the elegant Petit Palais (petitpalais.paris.fr). You'll miss out on the Mona Lisa, but you'll get works by Rembrandt, Rubens, Monet and more, in a building that's a work of art all by itself.

★ Swap Machu Picchu for Chavín de Huántar

Despite measures to control visitor numbers, the hikers keep on coming to Machu Picchu. In case you can't secure a trekking permit, there's more pre-Colombian magic at Chavín de Huántar – former capital of the Chavín people – and the lavishly decorated pyramid at Huacas del Sol y de la Luna near Trujillo; at either site, you'll get change from US$5 for entry.

★ Swap the Valley of the Kings for the Tombs of the Nobles

You'll battle with crowds to rival a pharaoh's funeral cortege to view the final resting place of Tutankhamun in Luxor's Valley of the Kings. For a more intimate experience, rent a bicycle and explore the rest of the West Bank – at the Tombs of the Nobles, a modest entry fee gains access to the lavishly painted tombs of later Egyptian nobles.

★ Swap the Taj Mahal for Delhi's Jama Masjid

The Taj may be the most beautiful building in the world, but entry is pricey and the crowds are phenomenal. To see medieval India without the headaches, head up the Grand Trunk Road to Delhi, where the free-to-enter Jama Masjid – India's largest mosque – swims with Mughal magic.

They can't charge for the view

It turns out Janet Jackson was right – the best things in life/travel are free, and that goes double for the views. Try these tips if you want the vistas without the price tag.

FREE VIEWPOINTS

There are steep entry fees to the observation decks of landmarks such as the Empire State Building and Burj Khalifa. For big views without the bucks, seek out government buildings, hilltop parks and harbour-fronts – you can't put a price on the free-to-access vistas from Tokyo's Metropolitan Government Building, Copenhagen's Christiansborg Palace or the summit of Hong Kong's Victoria Peak.

MIGHTY MONUMENTS

Seek out civic and religious monuments. Some of the most famous constructed sights in the world were built in lofty locations to catch the public gaze, with a mandate for free or low-cost public access. The only charge to climb Mt Rushmore is the fee for parking at the bottom, while the price of a ferry or metro ticket will get you to the hilltop Tian Tan Buddha on Hong Kong's Lantau Island.

TAKE A HIKE

Getting the best views often involves putting in a little legwork. Cities across the world are wrapped around lush, green spaces that have yet to be conquered by the urban sprawl. Hike in and you can bask in front of epic views for free and get a complimentary workout into the bargain. Sample a taste of what we mean at Vancouver's Stanley Park, London's Greenwich Park, Sydney's Observatory Hill Park or Singapore's Mt Faber Park.

CLIMB THE SPIRE

Most religious buildings are open to all-comers, and you can often climb to the rooftop for free (or for a nominal charge). Try taking in the view of old Cairo from the external staircase as you climb the minaret of Ibn Tulun Mosque; soak up the views of the University of Cambridge's colleges from atop Great St Mary's Church; or marvel at the giddying vistas from the top of Ulmer Münster in Germany.

FREE DAYS

Getting in for free is the ultimate travel hack. Tourist sites across the world offer free entry at certain times – a free afternoon, free entry an hour before closing, a free day once a month or once a year – so make sure you clock the cost-free times to come.

Educational sights

Sights with an educational angle, such as museums, art galleries and historic sites, are a rich vein to mine for free days. Scroll through opening times on venue websites, or Google 'free days' and the name of your chosen city. Even top-flight museums have free days – the Musée d'Orsay in Paris is free on the first Sunday of the month, while 14 July is free day at the Louvre.

Youth freebies

Always be on the lookout for free entry for young people or students – under 18s and EEA citizens aged 18-25 always get in free to the Louvre. And remember, some of the world's top museums are free all year – head to Washington DC and you can browse the 20 museums and one zoo run by the Smithsonian (si.edu) for free year-round.

National parks

Don't overlook national parks and other government-managed public lands. If you're travelling to the US, always check the annual calendar on the National Park Service website (nps.gov/planyourvisit/fee-free-parks.htm)

for the five national holidays when every national park in the US is free to visit. Always check the eligibility requirements – South Africa's fee-free National Parks Week in September is only open to South African citizens.

Free transport

Believe it or not, there are even free days on public transport. In 2022, Sydney announced 12 days of free travel to apologise for strike delays, while Germany set a fixed price of just US$9 for train fares across the country for three months. Over in Spain, free travel on trains run by Renfe (renfe.com) was extended into 2023. Sign up to news feeds for your chosen destination and see what gets announced.

Tips for stress-free sightseeing days

You've checked into your hotel and the sights are calling, but there are still pitfalls that could sink your perfect travel day. Here are our tips for hassle-free sightseeing.

Check that it's open

If you have your heart set on a particular sight or activity, do one final check before you set off to make sure it's open. Call ahead, or check the website, and make sure what you want to see is accessible – individual rooms often close for renovations, even if the rest of the museum or gallery stays open.

Make sure public transport is running

Engineering work and breakdowns can knock out transport lines, strikes are called with little warning, and bad – or even good – weather can cause cancellations. Always check public transport websites for travel warnings and have a plan B (like a rideshare bike or taxi app) for getting around.

Be weather-ready

Always check the weather before you head out. Turn your phone into a portable meteorological office with apps such as Accuweather (accuweather.com) and BBC Weather (bbc.co.uk/weather). Carry an umbrella or raincoat just in case – a '50% chance of rain' means it will probably rain a little, rather than it will be 100% dry or rainy.

Don't get lost

Before you set off for the day, drop a pin marking where you are staying on the Google Maps app, and leave more pins as you roam around, so you can retrace your steps. Make a mental note of landmarks and mark the spot where you parked your car or bicycle (or take a photo of your vehicle and the surroundings, so you can find it again easily).

Don't get caught short

Public toilets can be in short supply. Use the Flush toilet-finder app, or head to the nearest pub, fast-food restaurant or train station. Keep some change handy – the phrase 'spending a penny' hasn't really kept up with inflation.

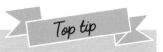

Top tip

"It's easy to execute a mini marathon while walking around the sights, so wear your comfiest pair of shoes. I always recommend trainers over formal shoes, boots, heels and sandals with uncovered toes. Pop a pair of lightweight flip-flops into your day pack if you're likely to be visiting sights where you need to take off your shoes, then change back to trainers for the tramp back to the hotel."

Joe Bindloss, travel writer

TAKE A DIGITAL DETOX

Don't let your overriding memories of your trip be of your phone screen. Turn off your devices and you'll get more from travel – try these digital detox hacks.

★ Camp out

Tent camping ticks multiple boxes. You'll be away from people and technology, you may not have a phone signal, you won't have electricity or a TV, and you'll have a ton of tasks to complete whenever you make or break camp. We suspect you won't even notice that you didn't have time to check the latest movements of the Kardashians.

★ Strip down your devices

You can't fritter away time on TikTok if you don't have the app. Before you leave, let folk know you're going offline, then remove those time-killer apps from your phone – or at least remove them from your home screen so you're less likely to be tempted.

★ Switch off your screens

You don't need to constantly check the news or emails, or stream the latest blockbuster on your laptop – particularly when you have the greatest show on Earth in front of you. Leave your laptop in the hotel so you aren't tempted to browse, and switch your phone to airplane mode to deter idle glances at social media.

★ Go off-grid

If you can't resist temptation, go cold turkey by staying somewhere without electricity – you'll be compelled to engage with your surroundings in a new way. This doesn't have to be a hardship; there are some gorgeous Robinson Crusoe beach getaways where being marooned from the modern world is exactly the point.

★ Go out device-free

Be brave. Leave all your tech in the hotel and step out into the destination with no distractions. Even better, bring a notepad and paper and write down what you are experiencing or draw some sketches. When you get back online, you'll find little has actually happened on those apps you check every five minutes.

How to enjoy a city for less

Cities eat money, but they also offer plenty of ways to save. Try these hacks to make your city breaks go further.

Find the free sights

Google 'free things to do' and the name of the city to find the free sights. Sightseeing cards can also get you places for free (or at least for less). Find more ideas in Lonely Planet's *The Best Things in Life Are Free*.

Stay cheaper

You'll always pay more for accommodation in the centre. Look for outlying suburbs with inexpensive places to stay and quick connections to the centre. Don't overlook Airbnb rooms or couch-surfing – these can be the cheapest digs in the city.

Be a midweek traveller

Come midweek and you'll avoid expensive minimum two-night stays and peak transport costs. If you must come at the weekend, see if any hotels in the business district offer discounts during their quiet time. Be wary of popular festivals and state holidays.

Take public transport

See if the city has a journey-planner website or app, and investigate passes for public transport – they're usually cheaper than individual tickets. Transport may cost less outside peak commuting hours. Check the time of the last bus or train to avoid a pricey cab ride.

Make the most of meal deals

Look out for discount set-lunches in the CBD on weekdays, or evening pre-theatre specials in the entertainment district. In diverse neighbourhoods, like London's Vietnamese quarter in Shoreditch, you can eat your way around the world on a shoestring.

Make your time count

Getting around a city takes time, so plan your days around individual districts. Plot must-see places to visit on the Google Maps app (google.com/maps) so you can see where the sights are clustered, and keep the map handy on your phone.

FIND A FREE TOUR

Local know-how will help you make sense of sights and scenery, and inexpensive tours are easy to find, from self-guided street-art circuits to seeing the sights for the cost of a tram ticket. Try these tips.

more than 130 destinations. There's no charge, and all the guides are friendly volunteers who want to show the best of their home city to outsiders.

Self-guided tours

Self-guided tours are a great way to see unseen sides of a city, and there's rarely a charge. Seek out free walking-tour maps in person at tourist offices or municipal information desks, or download routes in advance online. Access more user-generated tours on your smartphone via apps such as GPSMyCity (gpsmycity.com) and Geotourist (geotourist.com).

Let public transport be the tour

Plenty of overground public transport routes wind past the top sights, offering a tour for the price of a ticket. On Lisbon's 28 tram route, vintage streetcars trundle through the most historic city quarters, while Hong Kong's Star Ferry offers a small-change-priced tour of one of the world's most spectacular harbours.

Free guided tours

Free tours are more common than you think, particularly in well-trodden urban centres, though it's good form to give guides a tip. Volunteer guides run gratis tours in cities from London to Tokyo, offering maximum insights at minimum cost. Try major operators such as Freetour (freetour. com), Free Tours by Foot (freetoursbyfoot. com), Guru Walk (guruwalk.com) and Walkative (freewalkingtour.com).

Find a greeter

The International Greeter Association (internationalgreeter.org) puts visitors in touch with sociable locals who want to show off their city in

Bike or hike

Travel the slow way – on foot, or by bike – rather than jumping on public transport and you'll get a spontaneous city tour. Just pick two public transport stops in the city centre that are reasonably close together and use a city map to plot a route. You might be surprised at what you discover along the way.

Discount cards & other ways to save

Seeing the top attractions can cost big bucks if you leave everything until the last moment. Here are some top tricks for frugal sightseers.

Be an early booker

Tourist sights routinely offer discounts of 10% or more for advance bookings, particularly if you book online. Even if you don't book, always scan the entry prices online to see if there are any free-entry days or periods with cheaper tickets.

Grab a tourist card

Read the small print to be sure you really are getting a bargain, but city tourist cards such as the Omnia Vatican & Rome Pass (romeandvaticanpass.com) and the city cards offered by GoCity (gocity.com) offer free or discounted admission to the top sights – and often free public transport to get to them. Book online from abroad for additional discounts.

Annual-entry tickets

Many places offer annual memberships allowing unlimited entries, often for the price of a couple of visits. Check out annual passes from heritage bodies such as the UK's National Trust (nationaltrust.org.uk) and English Heritage (english-heritage.org.uk).

National park passes

Look out for annual passes at national parks – the US National Park Service's 'America the Beautiful' pass (nps.gov) covers entry to more than 2000 parks, refuges, forests and grasslands for just US$80. Find similar state-by-state passes in Australia, or see the 80-plus reserves overseen by South African National Parks with a Wildcard (sanparks.org/wildcard_new).

ACT YOUR AGE

Always be on the lookout for cut-price transport and discounted entry fees for students, young people and seniors. Check the rules before you come (some discounts are reserved for locals) and make sure you carry the right ID – if in doubt, bring your passport and any official cards from the institution where you are studying. An International Student Identity Card (ISIC) or International Youth Travel Card (IYTC) – isic.org – can save you money all over the place.

POCKET-FRIENDLY THRILL-SEEKING

"For low-cost hikes in the US, look for multi-state trails with sections outside the big national parks, such as the Appalachian Trail (appalachiantrail.org), where many parts of the trek can be accessed fee-free, and there's gratis camping in shelters and dispersed camping in the wild all along the trail."

Joe Bindloss,
travel writer

Bucket-list adventures, such as trekking and diving, can devour your travel budget, but there are low-cost thrills and spills if you know where to look.

Scuba diving

Ko Tao in Thailand is the undisputed world capital of discount diving. PADI dive certification courses here can cost as little as US$280 – a bona-fide bargain. For more low-cost diving, seek out dive spots with lots of competition between operators, such as the Philippines, the Red Sea and the Caribbean coast of Central America.

Surfing

With your own board, the world is one vast break, but prioritise countries with a laid-back scene and low-cost accommodation by the beach. Indonesia is the standout destination for intermediate surfers, while Sri Lanka is perfect for beginners, with cheap surf schools and board hire, budget stays and plenty of inland adventures for days when the breaks aren't performing.

Trekking

Easy answer – head to Nepal. Nowhere in the world offers so much variety and infrastructure at such low prices. El Chaltén in Argentina comes a close second. Save money by camping rather than staying in lodges, hiking or taking the bus to trailheads, and trekking through areas outside fee-charging national parks.

Rock climbing

With your own gear, rock climbing is free almost anywhere, but Railay near Krabi in Thailand stands out for the volume of routes and its cheap backpacker infrastructure. Elsewhere, seek out free national parks and public outcrops with low-cost camping nearby, such as Fontainebleau in France and England's Peak District.

Wildlife-watching

Seek out spots where wildlife spills beyond the national parks, such as Australia, where critters such as kangaroos and parrots are spotted around campgrounds and on rural roads. For African big game, Kenya and South Africa are the budget safari capitals, while Sri Lanka is top for cheap elephant encounters. The Pacific Coast of the US offers plenty of land-based whale-watching for free.

FAMILY TRAVEL HACKS

The tourist industry looks at small travellers and sees dollar signs, so be wise to the best ways to travel with tots in tow. Start with these tried and tested family hacks.

"'As a parent of three kids, I always travel with plenty of snacks (healthy and not) for those unforeseen delays, moments when everyone loses patience, or for an energy boost to get you to the next stop. Having a pack of cards, Uno or Dobble works well when you need to pass the time, and simple word-association games have helped us through many a long queue."

Imogen Hall, child therapist and writer

1 FAMILY ROOMS

Big families can mean big hotel bills, so bundle into one room to save. Most hotels can pop a spare single bed or cot into a double room, and many offer dedicated family rooms. If you can't fit into one room, get adjoining rooms, ideally with a linking door.

4 KID-FRIENDLY ATTRACTIONS

Museums, castles, activity centres, theme parks, swimming pools, zoos, aquariums and parks are top days out with kids. But small travellers have a low patience threshold. If you spend more than an hour at any site, fatigue can set in, so break often.

2 KEEP YOUR SCHEDULE LIGHT

Kids love new experiences, but not long journeys, disrupted mealtimes and walking in the heat. Plan rest stops and long lunch breaks, and be at the hotel in good time for dinner. Pause for a few days at each stop – kids won't want to leave the beach after a day.

5 HAVE A BACKUP PLAN

Long queues will strip the fun out of any family day out. If the line at the museum stretches around the block, consider bailing and creating an informal mini adventure by taking a fun form of public transport, like a river taxi, harbour ferry or old-fashioned tram.

3 STAY NEAR WATER

Kids aren't fussy if it's a hotel pool, a municipal pool, a river, a lake or the sea. Choose stays close to water to add instant fun to your trip and defeat the heat. If you rent a villa without a pool, a garden hose or sprinkler is a decent plan B.

6 CARRY INSTANT FUN

Bring along a diversion to distract kids during long waits – books, comics, card games, activity books, and drawing paper and pens are better options than putting the kids in front of a screen then fighting to get them off again.

7 FAMILY TICKETS

Most tourist sights offer family tickets that grant savings, though these are often aimed at a 1950s vision of the family – two adults, two kids. See if any city passes offer better discounts; some include free entry for up to two kids with each adult pass.

8 ENTRY PROMOTIONS

For attractions such as zoos, aquariums and theme parks, look for discount ticket promotions on cereals, snacks and soft drinks. Almost all require you to collect proof of purchase. Many sites offer promo tickets at quieter times of year or for early or late entry.

10 MEAL DEALS

Drinks and snacks can double the price of a day out, so keep your radar honed for kids' meals, which often come with drinks and dessert. If there's no kids' menu, order larger adult dishes and share. Packed lunches and free tap water are always your friends.

9 SCOOTERS, BAGS & BUGGIES

Many venues ask you to check in buggies, scooters and bags to reduce the risk of visitors bumping into that priceless Picasso, and there's often a charge. Leave bulky items in your hotel – a backpack carrier or baby sling is a solution for carrying smaller sightseers.

11 KEEPING TRACK OF TINY SIGHTSEERS

Ensure your kids are carrying your name and phone number, and run through an emergency drill covering what they need to do if you get separated. Tell them to contact an adult in uniform or someone at the ticket desk – and to stay in one spot so they're easier to find.

Rainy-day travel

If you can't beat the weather, embrace it. With these tricks, a rainy day doesn't have to put a dampener on your travels.

Shelter in a city

Big cities always have things to do in bad weather, from museums and galleries to covered markets and shopping malls. Bring a brolly for strolls between the sights, or travel by public transport to escape the damp and cold.

Rainy-day culture

If rain stops play, book a seat for a matinee at the theatre or take in a movie – perhaps a film in the local language for bonus cultural immersion? Plan B: head to the local library and grab some books on local culture.

Embrace getting wet

If you're getting wet anyway, it doesn't matter if it's raining. Swimming in the rain is a blast, so don't write off outdoor pools, lakes and rivers, and the sea. The same goes for kayaking, surfing, diving and other watersports.

Hole up with a book

Keep a book handy and you'll never be without something to do, no matter what the weather is doing. Find a space in the hotel lobby, your room balcony or a cafe, and slip into another world while the monsoon rages outside.

Defy the weather

If you have the right gear, the weather won't be an obstacle. Pack snow gear for winter travel (down jackets weigh little) and rainproofs for spring and autumn. You can even trek in the rain if you have a waterproof pack liner and a tent.

Make the weather the sight

Extreme weather can be a sight in itself. Tropical storms are spectacular from a safe vantage point, rainy weather is waterfall weather, and snow transforms every landscape into a thing of beauty.

ETHICAL ANIMAL INTERACTIONS

Always interact with wildlife in a way that ensures future generations can do it too. Here's the ethical way to connect with nature.

★ Choose an ethical operator

Always pick a tour operator or guide that follows ethical guidelines for interacting with animals. Never take elephant rides – it's proven to cause harm to these magnificent animals.

★ Meeting wildlife in the wild

Don't get too close to wild animals, for their safety as well as yours. Always obey the rules at national parks and wildlife reserves and seek out quieter zones, where wild animals can follow their natural behaviour without being corralled in by safari jeeps.

★ Feeding wild animals

Don't do it. Animals can become malnourished and habituated to humans, reducing their ability to survive in the wild and increasing the risk of conflicts between humans and wildlife. Instead of luring animals with food, wait by waterholes and other spots.

★ Captive creatures

Some zoos treat their animals more like prisoners. Be dubious of wildlife parks that offer the chance to hold wild animals. Only give your money to zoos that treat animals responsibly – small cages and enclosures with no natural greenery are big warning signs.

★ Whales & dolphins

Captive cetaceans are a definite no-no. When viewing whales and dolphins in the wild, choose operators that use small boats and insist on giving animals space rather than chasing down the pods.

★ Never buy animal products

Never buy souvenirs made from shells, coral, bones, teeth or other animal parts. Such items may also be banned under the Convention on International Trade in Endangered Species of Wild Fauna and Flora (cites.org), with severe penalties for import and export.

★ Support communities

To help animals, ensure your money also benefits local people in conservation areas, whether that's using homestays or hiring a guide from the local community.

BE A RESPONSIBLE TRAVELLER

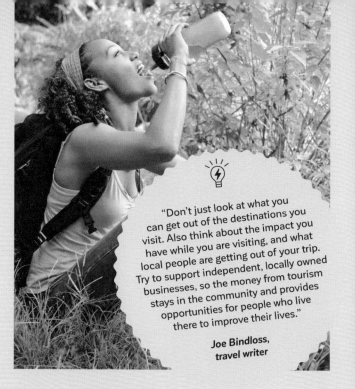

Savvy travellers contribute to local communities and leave a lighter mark when they visit. Prioritise slow travel and be open to paying a bit more for responsible experiences.

"Don't just look at what you can get out of the destinations you visit. Also think about the impact you have while you are visiting, and what local people are getting out of your trip. Try to support independent, locally owned businesses, so the money from tourism stays in the community and provides opportunities for people who live there to improve their lives."

Joe Bindloss,
travel writer

Watch your carbon footprint

If the only route in is by flying, offsetting your carbon emissions may help, but it's vastly better to emit less in the first place. Prioritise low-carbon transport – electric trains pollute less than diesel trains, buses pollute less (per person) than cars, and cycling or walking produces hardly any CO_2 at all. Avoid domestic flights unless there's no alternative – there will almost always be a train, bus or boat covering the same ground.

Be a responsible drinker

Travellers consume untold millions of drinks in disposable bottles – a major source of plastic pollution. Bring a sturdy water bottle or a trekking water bag and fill it up with purified water at your hotel, or purify your own with a filter or purification tablets. If you buy packaged drinks, cans and glass bottles are best – if there's a local recycling scheme, use it. Seek out hotels that purify their own water.

Watch your water usage

Huge amounts of energy and water are wasted washing towels at hotels – reuse the same towel throughout your stay unless it's actually dirty. When it comes to personal hygiene, showers use less water and energy than bathing in a tub. Always check how water is heated – if the only option is burning firewood, wash in cold water or skip the shower until you find somewhere that's heating water by using renewable energy.

Stay sustainably

Prioritise eco-hotels with tangible green policies, such as using renewable energy, recycling, growing their own produce, reusing wastewater and purifying their own drinking water, as well as employing local staff and supporting local community projects. Look for proof of claims of sustainability, such as certification from trusted organisations, such as EarthCheck (earthcheck.org).

Cut your consumption

Wherever you stay, turn off the fan, air-con or heating and any electrical appliances when you leave your room – it won't take long to heat up or cool down the room when you get back, and the planet will thank you. Think about the carbon miles of what you buy: an imported chocolate bar has more carbon emissions than a mango from a local market.

Clean up as you go

Not dropping litter goes without saying. It also costs nothing to pick up any litter you do find – if nothing else, you'll be setting a good example. Whenever you go trekking, carry a bag for rubbish and dispose of it properly when you get back to town. Look out for volunteer clean-up projects on beaches and trekking routes – no skills are needed and you'll make more of a difference than you would taking only photos and leaving only footprints.

Be animal aware

Wherever and whenever you interact with wildlife, consider your impact – potato chips are not what the coatimundis at Tikal in Guatemala need in order to be healthy, and harassing dolphins in their natural environment can cause harmful trauma to these vulnerable creatures. See p75 for further advice.

Choose ethical operators

Always check out the claims of responsible tour operators, as there's plenty of greenwashing out there. Seek out companies with green policies that conform to guidelines produced by environmental and conservation organisations, such as the Global Sustainable Tourism Council (gstcouncil.org). Intrepid Travel (intrepidtravel.com), G Adventures (gadventures.com) and Responsible Travel (responsibletravel.com) have solid reputations.

VOLUNTEER SMART

If you volunteer, investigate the organisation you're volunteering with. If it offers the chance to do whatever you want, whenever you want, it isn't prioritising the needs of local people. Seek longer-term placements that use your existing skills. Government-backed projects like the UK's International Citizen Service (volunteerics.org) and UN Volunteers (unv.org) are a good start.

STAY, YOUR WAY

WHERE TO STAY TO SAVE

Even the most expensive destinations have at least a few options for travellers who are watching the pennies. Start the accommodation search here...

> "Staying at a Sikh gurdwara in India is an amazing experience. Amritsar's Golden Temple offers inexpensive rooms and free dormitories for pilgrims, and you can eat for free at the langar (communal kitchen). Just make sure you leave a donation – the shrine has thousands of pilgrims to feed every day!"
>
> **Joe Bindloss,**
> **travel writer**

STAY IN A DORM

Always check out the local hostel scene and seek out new-style hostels with fun communal spaces, such as restaurants and bars (see p88). Hostels often have private rooms, but compare prices against cheap hotels, as there may be less expensive private rooms about. Find hostels worldwide through hostelworld.com and booking.com. Don't overlook the institutional but reliable hostels run by the Youth Hostel Association (yha.org.uk) and Hostelling International (hihostels.com).

PICK A LOCAL-STYLE HOTEL

Hotels targeting locals usually charge pocket-friendly prices, though these places can be a culture shock – or quite delightful, in the case of Japan's ryokan inns. South America is particularly well-stocked with guesthouses, known variously as *hospedajes, casas de huéspedes, residenciales, alojamientos* or *pensiones*. Also look out for *casas familiares* – family houses offering beds and home-cooked meals. There's the option to secure your door with a padlock, so bring your own for peace of mind.

FIND A COUCH

You don't need to rely on word of mouth or traveller noticeboards to find a comfy couch to surf on. Organised hospitality sites – such as couchsurfing. com, bewelcome.org and servas.org – connect sofa-surfers with couches, and hosts with guests who are up for a bit of cultural exchange. Sites typically charge a membership fee, but stays are free.

CAMP OUT

Whether you sleep under canvas or in a camper van or RV, camping is almost always the cheapest way to stay. You won't find many camping sites in the city centre, but they're plentiful around hiking routes, touristy coastlines and on the edges of country towns on the tourist trail – see p86 and p90 for plenty of tips.

HOME SWAPPING & HOUSESITTING

Letting a stranger stay in your home can open doors to strangers returning the favour, and it's usually free, although it's often a longer-term option, rather than the odd night here and there – check out Home Exchange (homeexchange.com) and Love Home Swap (lovehomeswap.com) to get started. Option B is housesitting – where you pay for your stay by watching over someone's home (maybe cleaning and feeding the pets). Find stays online at MindMyHouse (mindmyhouse.com) and House Carers (housecarers.com).

 ## STAY RURAL

In rural areas, 'homestay' usually means staying with a working family – a great way to steer tourist income to rural communities. Some countries have national homestay schemes, such as Nepal's Community Homestay programme (communityhomestay.com) and Italy's agriturismi (agriturismo.it). Alternatively, find homestays worldwide at homestay.com and bedycasa.com. If you don't mind getting your hands dirty, World Wide Opportunities on Organic Farms (wwoof.net) arranges free working stays at organic farms worldwide.

 ## RENT A ROOM OR FLAT

Airbnb (airbnb.com) has revolutionised the room-renting business – and upset many local renters. Nevertheless, it's a way to find cheap accommodation to rent by the night or week, including properties that house big groups and families. Homestay.com is another similar option. Always check the fine print for extra charges for cleaning and bedding.

 ## STAY IN STUDENT DIGS

Many universities offer student rooms for rent during the holidays, translating to a bargain stay in a great part of town for cheap food and nightlife. University Rooms (universityrooms.com) has digs everywhere, from Montréal to the historic colleges of Oxford and Cambridge. Also look out for uni rooms on booking.com.

RELIGIOUS STAYS

Enquire at religious centres for inexpensive overnight accommodation. In Christian countries, that might be a monastery or a Christian retreat; in diverse India, it might be a Sikh gurdwara or a Hindu ashram. You may be able to stay for free, though a donation is appropriate, and there may be rules about abstaining from alcohol, smoking and even sex. Start the search for monastic stays at monasteries.com, monasterystays.com and Goodnight & God Bless (goodnightandgodbless.com).

Pay less for your room

Even if you decide to stay in a five-star hotel or resort, the same room can still cost a little or a lot, depending on how, where and when you book. Here are some handy ways to save.

Book early, book direct

Dynamic pricing is the norm at posher hotels, so you'll pay less at quiet times. Book at least six months ahead to secure a room for a reasonable rate in touristy hubs. Don't assume booking sites offer the best deals – you may do better by approaching a hotel directly. Off-season discounts are easy to snag at quiet times, even at budget hotels, and walk-in rates can drop luxe rooms down to midrange prices.

Last-minute deals

Late deals are easier to find for hotel rooms than for flights. Bigger hotels book out blocks of rooms for tour agencies, releasing any leftover rooms about 24 hours before arrival. If you're flexible, try on the day – if guests don't claim their rooms, hotels may re-release these rooms at around 6pm, so it's always worth making a call around this time.

Stay out of season

There are fewer cheap rooms around in the tourist season, when hotels have no problem filling more expensive classes. For a guaranteed low rate, come out of season – the weather might be patchy, but rates can plummet, except during mini-peaks such as over the Christmas break. Rates also go up and down on a weekly cycle – look for cheap deals midweek, or at weekends in the business district.

"Hotel room rates change frequently and sometimes even go down a few nights before your arrival. Book a fully refundable or cancellable rate and keep checking to see if it gets lower. Leverage hotel loyalty points – when booking a room on points, you don't have to pay taxes, sometimes knocking 20% or more off the price."

Scott Mayerowitz, head of editorial at The Points Guy (thepointsguy.com)

Skip unneeded perks

If you don't need a full breakfast, why pay for it? Most hotels offer free coffee and tea in your room and you'll almost always pay less for a croissant in town. If you have a smartphone and a local data SIM, you probably don't need Wi-Fi, and hotel laundry services usually cost more than a service wash at a laundrette.

Be a loyal customer

Most of the big hotel chains have loyalty schemes that can quickly add up to free stays. Check in with big players, such as Marriot, Hilton, IHG and Hyatt, to see what incentives they offer for new sign-ups – at the least, you might get a free breakfast or a room upgrade. Sites such as booking.com and hotels.com have their own membership schemes for loyal bookers, earning cheaper rates or free stays.

Use unused bookings

Roomer (roomertravel.com) acts as a marketplace for the resale of unused, non-refundable hotel bookings, offering big discounts on full-price rates. There's a fee, but it will handle changing the booking into your name, so you can rock up like the room was yours all along.

Use your points

Credit card points can be a very cost-effective way to book hotel rooms, particularly if you qualify for 'Elite Status' on a card linked to a hotel loyalty scheme. Look for cards that offer a hefty points bonus for new members – in the US, the Chase Sapphire Preferred card (chase.com) is a local legend, but you'll need to run plenty of costs through your card for the top perks.

© JONATHON STOKES / LONELY PLANET; THE SAFARI COLLECTION

TIPS TO GET A TASTE OF THE HIGH LIFE

★ **Going all-out**
Travel isn't all about scrimping and saving. If you're looking for a truly luxurious stay, consider these tips:

★ **Stay plush**
Don't waste the experience of staying somewhere fabulous by picking an ordinary room; get the best class of room you can afford, ideally in club class, so you get a decent view and perks such as free snacks and drinks and a butler service.

★ **Stay special**
Modern luxury hotels can look a bit samey – seek out something special, like a hotel in a converted maharaja's palace or a room with visiting wildlife in Kenya's Giraffe Manor (thesafaricollection.com).

★ **Make the most of it**
Get your money's worth from those indulgent five-star facilities – arrive as early as you're allowed and make the most of the freebies. If there's a complimentary drink, quaff it. If there's free use of the sauna, get your steam on.

HOTEL ROOM HACKS

OK, so you've secured your room at the perfect price. Here's how to make the most of your stay.

★ Beware the minibar

The mark-up for minibar drinks can be eye-watering, so consider grabbing some takeouts from a local shop (you can always pop them in the minibar fridge to keep them cool). If you run out of drinking water in your room, there's normally a supply of free drinking water in the gym.

★ Dare you call room service?

Check the prices for room-service meals and snacks before you order – you may be better off ordering a takeaway meal via UberEats or a local delivery service and picking it up in front of the hotel.

★ Check the switches

Hotel light switches and sockets are tucked away in mysterious places, so ask where everything is when

you are first shown to your room. When you leave, check all the sockets to make sure you haven't left any chargers behind.

★ Be adaptable

If you forget to bring an adaptor for the local plug sockets, reception can normally provide one for a deposit. As a plan B, look on the back of the TV – there may be a USB socket that you can use to charge your devices.

★ Keep the power on

Many hotels have a master switch for the electricity, operated by your room keycard. If you need to keep charging your devices, any plastic card will usually activate the switch, but turn off the lights and air-con to save energy.

★ Always lock up

Always lock your door before you go to sleep, as well as when you go out. Also keep the windows closed – monkeys are legendary for making daring hotel-room raids in search of eatables.

★ Keep your stuff safe

If there isn't an in-room safe, ask reception to look after any particularly valuable items. If you leave valuables in your bag, keep it locked to discourage casual pilferers. Don't 'hide' things under your pillow – use a sock tucked into your shoe instead.

Renting a villa for beginners

Renting a villa or apartment can be a great way to cut your overheads and you may get somewhere to park as part of the deal. Here are our top villa hacks.

Finding a villa

Thousands of websites and agencies can help you find the villa of your dreams, but many properties are out of the centre, so you may need a hire car or a working knowledge of local bus routes. Agencies usually charge a commission – try vrbo.com, holidaylettings.co.uk, flipkey.com and clickstay.com to connect with villa owners without paying a fee.

Does it have to be a villa?

Airbnb is great for finding apartments and homes for rent – you probably won't get a pool, but you will find some great city-centre locations. Be aware that many places charge by the night, not the week; bring costs down by sharing with a group. For families, a two-bedroom apartment can be a bargain compared with paying for multiple hotel rooms.

Ways to save

Think about the features you actually need. A pool is a nice touch, but you'll get more for your money if the pool is shared, or if you go without. Outdoor space also comes at a premium – if you'll be out most of the time, do you really need a garden? Give some thought to bedrooms too – many one-bedroom properties have a fold-out bed in the lounge, making space for four. If there's a charge for cleaning and bedding, you may be able to save by bringing your own towels and sheets.

Booking tips

Travel in the shoulder or low season for low prices and better availability, and book early. Always ask if there's any chance of a discount out of season. France has a good system of gîtes (holiday cottages), but the French book early, particularly during school holidays – start looking online at least six months in advance at gites-de-france.com, gitelink.com and gites.com.

Camping or glamping?

Sleeping under canvas can be truly liberating, or truly demoralising if you time it wrong and it rains every day. Here are some top hacks to help you stay a happy camper.

Tent or RV?

Vehicle spaces cost more than tent spaces and you'll pay extra to hook up to water and electricity – going back to basics with a tent is a great way to save. Do you even need a tent? Plenty of campgrounds offer both barebones camping spaces and comfy glamping stays, in everything from yurts and shepherds' huts to treehouses – usually for less than the price of a hotel room. If you do go down the RV route, bring a bicycle; campgrounds are often miles from the centre, and you don't want to have to break camp every time you need to pop to the shops.

"Avoid camping in fields. Even if they seem empty in the evening, you might find your dreams interrupted at dawn by a herd of cows and an annoyed farmer! Be very careful about lighting a fire. Sometimes there are rules against this, and in the middle of a hot summer the forest-fire risk can make lighting fires very dangerous."

Stuart Butler, travel writer and avid outdoors enthusiast (stuartbutlerjournalist. com)

Wild camping or campground?

Wild camping is (usually) free, but it's not allowed everywhere, so check the local rules and ask before you pitch. You'll also have the problem of finding drinking water and dealing with toilet stops. At a campground, there'll be showers, toilets and often a kitchen and a kids' play area. Find sites using the likes of pitchup.com, park4night.com, acsi.eu, searchforsites.co.uk and campercontact.com.

Tent tips

Golden rule No 1: carry a mallet, and use heavy-duty tent pegs made of steel, not bendy aluminium. Find a flat, level and dry area, clear any loose sticks or pebbles and start setting up well before sunset. Nobody likes a soggy tent; give yours an extra coating of waterproofing spray before you head out, and practise putting it up and taking it down, so you don't have to work it out for the first time in a gale.

Sleep comfortably

For a good night's sleep, lift yourself up off the cold, hard ground – carry a roll-up foam mat or inflatable sleeping mat. Sleeping bags should be able to match the conditions: one- and two-season bags are only good for summer; you'll need four or five seasons if the temperature dips below freezing. Tuck the clothes for the morning into the bottom of your bag and you'll have a pre-heated outfit for the morning.

Manage the microclimate

Most tents have ventilation flaps, so use them. The mesh will let the damp air you exhale escape, reducing the chance of a tent dripping with condensation. Never cook inside your tent – water vapour is guaranteed. If you don't have a hot-water bottle, fill your drinking water bottle and tuck it into a sock (you'll also have a bottle of fresh water for the morning).

Keep out uninvited guests

Be pest smart – keep the openings of your tent zipped up at night to deter mosquitoes and crawly critters drawn in by your lantern. The smell of food can draw rats and other small beasts from miles around, so put rubbish in bins, wash up promptly and keep food in sealed bags or plastic tubs. To keep rodents out of your RV, leave cotton-wool balls soaked in peppermint oil around potential entry points.

CAMPING HACKS FOR TREKKERS

Unless you have access to a yak or packhorse, keep the load light. Camping gear should be pared down to a minimum – if it's hot, can you get by with a hammock and a mosquito net? If it's cold, leave out unnecessary items (surplus electronics, that weighty novel) to make space for a decent sleeping bag and an emergency survival bag. Bring your own water purification system and you won't have to haul too much drinking water; a liquid-fuel-powered Whisperlite-style pump stove will save weight compared with one powered by propane cannisters.

Things to look for in a great hostel

Some hostels are basic boxes, some are lavish, but all offer that sweet-spot combination of cheap beds and social interaction. Here's what to look for in a great hostel.

 ### CLEAN DORMS

It goes without saying that dorms should be clean and well looked after. Prices fall as the number of beds goes up; smaller dorms with four or six beds offer a quieter night's sleep. Single-sex dorms or women-only hostels are safer for female travellers. Read traveller reviews to get a feel for the hostel's vibe.

 ### SECURE LOCKERS

If you're sharing dorm space, you need somewhere secure to keep your stuff, rather than relying on the honesty of fellow dorm-mates. Most hostels provide lockers, but bring your own padlock for peace of mind, even if the hostel provides one. Keep the key on a hairband around your wrist so you don't lose it.

 ### BETTER BEDS

Bunks should be sturdy and comfy – you don't want to be woken up by creaks from the top bunk (bring earplugs and an eye mask). Many travellers aim for the top deck, but if you nab the bottom bunk, you can create privacy by tucking the edge of a spare sheet under the mattress above. In case the sheets aren't 100% spotless, bring a sleeping-bag liner.

 ### CLEAN BATHROOMS

Always check the bathroom before you decide to stay. Mould on the grout, cubicle doors that don't lock and sticking plasters in the shower tray are warning signs. Better hostels have a separate bathroom for every dorm. Hostel showers are one of the natural homes of the wild verruca – carry flip-flops to keep your feet germ-free.

WI-FI

Most hostels provide it, though speeds can be sluggish, bandwidth limited, and connections may not be secure (use a VPN). Consider getting a local data SIM for your mobile for in-room browsing. If there's no Wi-Fi, see if there are computer terminals for checking email, and use them cautiously (see p101).

"When looking for a hostel, find a place that matches your travel style. There are party hostels, social hostels, quiet hostels, eco hostels, boutique hostels...the list goes on. So, if you're heading to Krakow to party the night away, be sure to stay in a hostel where this kind of behaviour is welcome (and encouraged!) and not a laid-back, quiet hostel, where everyone is in bed by 10pm."

Matt Kepnes, globe-trotting blogger and founder of nomadicmatt.com

A COMMON ROOM

Part of the fun of hostelling is connecting with other travellers, and there should be somewhere for this to happen: a breakfast room, roof terrace, dining hall, games room or old-fashioned TV room. Get talking – the traveller grapevine is a treasure trove of travel tips.

A SHOP

Not a deal breaker, but having somewhere on-site where you can buy drinking water, snacks, beers and toilet paper can be handy for your late-night arrival or to stock up before an early morning departure.

A CAFE

An increasingly common feature of modern hostels is cheap eats to match the cheap sleeps. Food tends to be traveller fare rather than authentic local food, but vegetarian and vegan options are easy to find. If there's no cafe, Uber Eats, Just Eat and the like can deliver your fast food of choice to the front door.

A BAR

The world's top hostels offer on-site drinking, often on the rooftop, with views over the city. Promotions on house drinks are common, but keep an eye on your bar bill, as it's easy to get chatting and spend more than the cost of your dorm bed on a night in.

A KITCHEN

Self-catering is a great way to reduce your overheads – make sure the fridge and cooker are clean, and get to the kitchen early at mealtimes. Travelling with a cooking pan and a sharp knife can save waiting in queues. Carry a roll of white stickers and a marker pen to label your food, and always do your washing up – hostelling requires mutual respect.

MAKE YOUR VEHICLE YOUR HOME

Plenty of travellers avoid the hassle of finding a hotel by making their vehicle into a mobile home, whether that means a mattress in the back of a station wagon, or a fully equipped recreational vehicle. Consider these tips...

★ Crunch the costs

Sleeping in your own wheels means inexpensive accommodation and easier transport, but it won't always be the cheapest option. Draw up a spreadsheet of likely costs – and remember to account for fuel, vehicle taxes, insurance, road tolls, maintenance costs and parking – so you can compare against the costs of going by public transport and staying in hotels. Remember, you can always rent a vehicle for a few days if you need one.

★ Choosing your wheels

Renting a vehicle is less hassle, but buying means you don't have to worry so much about scratching the paintwork. Consider the roads you'll be driving – if your route involves unsurfaced roads, you'll need a 4WD and decent clearance under the vehicle. Choose a vehicle that's common in the destination, so you can easily find spare parts at breakers yards. Fords,

Toyotas and Volkswagens are usually a safe bet.

★ Kitting out your vehicle

The sky is the limit when it comes to customising your vehicle for overland travel. As a bare minimum, you'll need a bed or mattress, somewhere to store water, and a way to keep food cool, whether that's a battery-powered fridge or an ice-cooled cold box. Ample storage is essential – stackable plastic storage boxes are the easiest option, but use straps

to hold them in place. See p50 for more tips.

★ Renting a motorhome

Plenty of countries have specialist motorhome rental companies. Britz (britz.com) and maui (maui-rentals.com) are famous operators in Australia, New Zealand and South Africa; in the US and Canada, try Cruise America (cruiseamerica.com) or CanaDream (canadream. com). The camperdays.com search engine can help you find companies around the world.

★ Going by car

A car will almost always cost less to buy/rent and run than a van, and with smaller engines and better fuel economy, they tend to be less thirsty too. If you plan to sleep in the vehicle, you'll need the large boot area of an estate car or station wagon and a foam mattress. Bring a pop-up tent so you have choices – a rooftop TentBox (tentbox.com) will give you the best of both worlds. Bring

> "Sleeping in your car is possible, but it's frowned on in campgrounds and holiday parks, so bring a tent as a backup. Sleeping by the roadside comes with risks – including being woken up and breathalised by the police! Don't assume you can stop overnight in parking areas, unless there's a sign saying it's permitted."
>
> **Joe Bindloss, travel writer**

a good sleeping bag or blankets to stay warm – leaving the ignition and heating on is an easy way to drain your battery.

★ Campground perks

For major perks such as showers, toilets, drinking water, cooking facilities and somewhere to empty your toilet waste tanks and bins, look for dedicated campgrounds and holiday parks along the coast and around the city limits in tourist areas. Most have dedicated areas for camper vans and RVs, with water supplies and electricity hookups to avoid draining your battery. If you're overlanding in Africa, hotels and safari lodges may let you camp in the grounds for a fee.

★ Mobile home safety

Vehicles are easy to break into, or steal, so have some hiding places for your valuables, and try to park overnight in supervised parking areas, such as campgrounds or rest areas. If the area seems dodgy, consider booking into a

hotel for the night so you can bring your valuables inside and park in the hotel car park. If you visit remote areas or drive in winter, bring enough food, water and blankets, and a phone for emergencies (and a way to charge it).

REST BY THE ROADSIDE

For long highway journeys, check if you can stop at roadside rest areas. France has an extensive system of *aires* – dedicated (and usually free) rest areas for motorhomes at motorway services and along country roads, with basic facilities such as water supplies and drains, but rarely toilets. In Germany, they're known as *stellplatze*; in Italy, the term is *area di sosta*. In New Zealand, look out for 'Freedom Camping' signs. Find rest stops easily using apps such as park4night (park4night.com) and Campercontact (campercontact.com).

© JUSTIN FOULKES / LONELY PLANET

TRAVEL TO EAT (& DRINK)

The best meals for the lowest prices

For many people, travel is about eating, and paying a bargain price is the wasabi on the sashimi. Here's how to get more from your food budget.

GO BIG FOR BREAKFAST

It's the most important meal of the day, but hotel buffets can be pricey – seek out authentic local breakfasts, such as newspaper-sized dosas (rice and lentil pancakes) in India, steak and eggs in the US, soy milk with *youtiao* (savoury doughnut strips) in China or the heart-stopping full English breakfast.

BALANCE LUNCH & DINNER

You don't want to sacrifice too much sightseeing time to long, lingering lunches, and lavish suppers will scythe through your budget, so mix it up. Set lunches are a bargain way to fill up, but save the big spreads for days when you can kick back and relax. On sightseeing days, have lunch quickly – say a sandwich, wrap or burger – then settle in for a big three-course dinner later, when it won't cost you valuable museum time.

GRAZE ON THE STREETS

Don't feel confined by the strictures of three meals a day. In many countries, street food is abundant, cheap and tasty, so you can let your taste buds rather than your stomach dictate when to eat. A typical meal spread might be a 6am snack, a mid-morning fried rice, soup for lunch and a prolonged evening of grazing, starting when the night markets open. To stay healthy, mix up rich foods with seasonal fruit from street-side stalls.

MEALS IN TRANSIT

Some trains have dining cars, some boats have cafes and some buses stop for roadhouse bites, but not all, so be prepared. For early starts, grab drinks and snacks that don't need to be chilled, or ask the hotel if they can provide a packed breakfast. Get to the station an hour early so you have time to buy some food to go – there'll usually be somewhere nearby selling packed-to-travel meals that are more nourishing than potato chips.

EAT HOW THE OTHER HALF EAT

Everyone wants to be able to tell the folks back home that they ate the best meal in town, but that doesn't always mean Michelin stars. Try these tips for roaming gourmands.

The Michelin set

Michelin stars (guide.michelin.com) have become the benchmark for restaurant quality, but they also push up prices and demand for tables. Book far ahead for restaurants with star appeal, such as triple-starred Pierre Gagnaire (pierregagnaire.com) in Paris. Don't overlook restaurants that have lost a Michelin star – you'll still get quality and perhaps a lower price. To maximise your choices, hit cities with multiple Michelin-starred restaurants, such as Tokyo or Spain's Donostia-San Sebastián.

Hotel fine dining

Many of the world's top restaurants are found in the top hotels, and guests often get priority access. If you're in the mood for a slap-up hotel dinner, check the dress code and reserve at least a few days ahead to avoid missing out. If you stay full-board, check which restaurants you are covered for – sometimes the meals included only cover less posh buffet restaurants on the premises.

Top-class street food

You don't need a white tablecloth to enjoy the best meal in town. Singapore's Hill Street Tai Hwa Pork Noodle received a Michelin star for its superior, pocket-priced noodles with minced pork. Across town, Liao Fan Hong Kong Soya Sauce Chicken Rice & Noodle lost its star, but still attracts a loyal following for its world-class soya-sauce chicken.

Other cities where fine diners swing by for street food include Hong Kong, Bangkok, Delhi, Tokyo, Marrakesh, İstanbul and Mexico City.

Eating with atmosphere

If you can't eat with the high-fliers, eat somewhere with atmosphere. A dinner of wave-fresh kingfish on the sand will probably linger longer in your memory than being charged US$100 for a thimbleful of steak tartare with seagrass foam. Seek out al fresco dining on cobbled market squares in Europe and South America, mom-and-pop diners in the rural US, night market meals in Asia, outdoor barbecues in Africa and beachfront seafood shacks anywhere with sand.

How to always get a table

Don't be the person who planned a trip around a Michelin-starred restaurant and didn't get a table. Here are our tips for securing the top tables in town.

Reserve ahead

For the Geraniums, Benoits and Eleven Madison Parks of this world, you'll need to book months in advance, so call ahead when planning your trip so you know how early to book. Ask politely, don't demand, and let them know you're flexible. If there's no table for 8pm, could they squeeze you in for a late seating at 9.30pm? If there are no tables, could they fit you in at the bar?

Dine early or late

Eating has its own rush hour, and tables may suddenly come free if you book outside of this primetime slot. Early dining is becoming increasingly common, so the 6pm to 8pm window is getting increasingly congested – book for 9pm or later and you'll stand a much better chance.

"Don't get too hung up on one particular restaurant – many top chefs run multiple venues. Don't overlook the protégés of big-name chefs; when someone who worked under Gordon Ramsay or Alain Ducasse sets up on their own, their new enterprises are always worth checking out."

**Joe Bindloss,
travel writer**

Get a better table

There's a hierarchy for tables, so make a good impression when you arrive to avoid being plonked at the back by the bathrooms. If the dress code is smart, dress smart; look like you belong and you'll almost always get a prime spot.

Go on the wait list

If the restaurant doesn't take bookings, you may be able to get your name added to a waiting list for a table on the day. Swing by earlier than you plan to eat – an hour should do it – then see how long you'll have to wait (there'll normally be a bar nearby where you can pass the time).

Ask your hotel concierge

The old-school concierges depicted in *The Grand Budapest Hotel* are a dying breed, so don't expect hotel staff to get you a table in a full restaurant. What they can do is help you make a booking (and raise your chances of getting a good table), or direct you to another dining choice if the dinner of your dreams is out of reach.

EAT LIKE A LOCAL

The tourist version of local dishes can be insipid and bland. These tips will set you on the right path to flavours as flamboyant as an Easter fiesta.

★ Read ahead

Make a point of checking out local papers and dining guides for tips on the hottest tables in town. Before you arrive, read up on the local delicacies – some, like Brunei's sago-gloop *ambuyat* or Iceland's rotten shark *hákarl* take some getting used to, so it pays to have an inkling of what to expect.

★ Eat where the locals eat

It's easy to spot the best places to eat – they're packed out with locals rather than tourists and there's a queue every mealtime. Often, the menu and sign will be in the local language, so be ready to order by pointing to what you see displayed on the counter, or on other patrons' plates.

★ Browse the markets

Identify what is going into local cook pots at the local market (particularly the fruit and vegetable section and the pungent 'wet market' selling fresh meat and fish). Ask stallholders the names of top-selling ingredients and make a point of ordering dishes that include them.

★ Eat on the streets

To plug into the local street-food scene, head to the clusters of food stalls at transport hubs, hawker courts and night markets, or the business district at lunchtime. The usual rules apply: busy stalls are busy for a reason; quiet stalls are quiet for a reason.

★ Be ambitious

Be brave and order things you wouldn't normally consider, and you'll enter a new world of tastes and sensations. Don't think too hard about where ingredients have come from – assess dishes in terms of flavours and textures and you may be pleasantly surprised.

★ Be a region-ivore

Make it a mission to try regional delicacies. Ask locals about the must-trys in the area, and the best places to try them. That might involve a trip to an off-piste corner of town for a meal that you'll be talking about for years.

THERE IS SUCH A THING AS A CHEAP LUNCH

Around the world, dinner comes dear while lunch comes cheap. Restaurants across the world lay on special deals at lunchtime, so fill up in the middle of the day to save.

"In the Middle East, the best lunch spots are often clustered around covered bazaars or in busy street markets. These places sometimes offer table seating, but more often sell food to go, catering for bazaar workers and customers. Many have been in existence for generations and the best ones are always busy – just follow the locals."

Virginia Maxwell,
travel writer and Middle East
and Turkey expert

Food markets

Night markets and hawker courts abound in Asia, but don't overlook the stalls around produce markets in Europe, Oceania and the Americas. Alongside fresh ingredients, you'll find plenty of stands selling filling, portable lunches – burgers, tacos, pizza slices – at lower than restaurant prices. And don't disregard the encampments of food trucks that gather close to touristy areas, business districts and festivals.

Graze the buffet

A buffet meal probably won't include the gourmet version of every dish on the table, but you can certainly fill up for a bargain price – or at least, a bargain price for so much nourishment. Find buffets at tourist restaurants, resorts and family hangouts where locals gather for a slap-up Sunday lunchtime feed. Don't have an active afternoon planned – it's easy to go overboard when it's all-you-can-eat.

Set menus

Set menus come in all shapes and sizes, but at lunch, the focus is normally on a starter and a main. Dishes are normally crowd-pleasers and you'll typically get a choice of main courses with a local starch source – rice, noodles, bread, potatoes, polenta and friends – plus a starter, soup or salad, and maybe a drink. The bill can sometimes be less than a single main course.

Eat fast food

While you probably don't want to live off fast food (think of *Super Size Me*), it has its place as a cheap, fast meal before you jump on a bus or train. Remember, fast food doesn't have to mean international chains – seek out local fast-food joints, and trade the pizzas and burgers for dishes that resonate with locals.

© 4KODIAK / GETTY IMAGES

Have a picnic

The cheapest lunch anywhere is the one you assemble yourself. Head to the nearest market or deli, grab some bread, cheese, charcuterie, patisserie, fruit and salad vegetables for a lunch in a local park. In Asia, seek out portable snacks such as *nasi lemak* (coconut rice in banana leaves) in Malaysia; *lamprais* (rice and sauces) in Sri Lanka; or samosas (spiced pastry parcels) in India.

Hit the bakery

Bakeries don't just sell bread and sticky buns. You can almost always find something savoury to munch on, from meaty stuffed pastries to pizza slices, sandwiches, and the fuel-for-workers classic bacon baguette. You'll fill up cheaply, but grab some fruit to cut through the grease.

Eat like a worker

Workers' cafes can fill you up to the gills for a song almost anywhere in the world. Look for cheap cafes around places where working people gather, such as street markets and transport hubs, and order what the locals are eating.

Have a religious experience

In many cultures, religious centres lay on free food for pilgrims, though a donation is usually appropriate. In India, seek out temples run by the International Society for Krishna Consciousness (ISKCON), or the special pilgrim kitchens known as *langars* at Sikh gurdwaras. In Buddhist countries, many feast days at monasteries and temples feature free food for all, funded by donations – if you hear about a local temple festival, always check it out.

KNOW THE LINGO

Every country has its own terms for a set lunch. In Francophone countries, look for *cartes de midi* or *formules déjeuner* menus, or chalkboards offering the *plat du jour* (dish of the day). In Spanish-speaking lands, key words are *menú del día* or *menu executive*. Asia has many variations on the thali – a plate meal with rice or flatbreads and multiple sauces. In Sri Lanka, look for 'rice and curry'; in Malaysia and Indonesia, track down *nasi kandar* or *nasi campur*.

Food hygiene 101

That delectable-looking street food is endlessly enticing, but will it make you sick? Worry no longer – here are some easy travel hacks to keep Delhi belly from the door.

"In countries where hygiene can be dodgy, many travellers go vegetarian for the duration of the trip to reduce the risk. In South Asia, look out for restaurant signs saying 'veg' or 'pure-veg'; in Southeast Asia, seek out traveller-oriented vegetarian places or Buddhist restaurants for hygienic vegetarian food."

Joe Bindloss, travel writer

★ Ice? No dice!

Unless you're 100% certain of the source of the water used to make ice, avoid it. Bottled drinks can be refrigerated without any need for cubes of dubious origin, and it's easy to decline ice when it's offered. If you absolutely insist on ice, stick to upmarket restaurants and international fast-food chains.

★ Ice cream, eggs & dairy

Ice cream and other milk products can be dodgy – skip ice cream unless you're sure it hasn't been defrosted and refrozen. Avoid unpasteurised milk and uncooked eggs to avoid salmonella, E.coli, listeria and campylobacter. If you need a safe dairy fix, curd can boost your natural gut fauna.

★ Fish & seafood

How far are you from the sea? Anything over 160km (100 miles) in a tropical country and you're edging into food-poisoning territory. Always consider the freshness of fish and seafood before you order. Many restaurants display their fish on ice so you can assess the condition – sliminess, a dull colour, a strong smell and cloudy, sunken eyes are warning signs.

★ Meat & chicken

Well-cooked red meat is usually safe to eat, but be wary of raw meat dishes unless locals are tucking in without problems, and avoid dishes that have been left sitting around at room temperature. Chicken is more risky – always cut pieces open before you bite in to make sure it's cooked through.

★ Fruit & salads

Avoid salads and pre-cut fruit unless you're sure they've been washed in purified water. If you buy your own, peel them or wash them yourself and munch in confidence. Juices are another risky proposition – what was the source of the water or ice?

★ Rice

We're serious! Reheated rice can be a gamble, as some of the bacteria that grow on rice create toxins that are not destroyed by heating.

SELF-CATER IN STYLE

Renting a room, apartment or villa with a kitchen can cut your dining costs – or at least give you options when you can't be bothered to go out for dinner. Try these tips for self-caterers.

Self-catering essentials

Self-catering kitchens come with a basic cooking kit – pans, a colander, chopping board, plates, bowls, cups and cutlery – but really sharp knives are rare, as are place settings for more than four people, and appliances can be temperamental. Essentials to pack include a bottle opener, a lighter (in case the hob won't light), a lightweight tin opener, and a small, sharp knife. Also pack a torch for finding the electrical consumer unit if the power trips.

A basic cooking kit

Self-catering cupboards are full of abandoned, half-full packets, so you can often find enough to throw together a meal on the first night, but always carry a basic condiment kit of salt, pepper, sugar and cooking oil, so you don't have to buy big packets that you won't finish. Tea and coffee are also useful things to have in your stash. On your way to the accommodation, grab milk, dry pasta and something to put on top of it,

just in case; wine is optional, but recommended, to toast your new (temporary) home.

Grill the owner (not literally)

Make sure the owner provides detailed instructions about how things work, including the electricity, gas, water, door locks, heating and – critically – the cooker. Do not leave this until you arrive, as many places just leave the key for you in a combination lockbox, so there'll be nobody to ask.

Be ready to barbecue

If possible, book somewhere with outdoor space, even if it's just a terrace or balcony. Barbecuing is a great way to make a meal with minimum preparation and without too many leftovers. If the accommodation doesn't have a barbecue, buy an inexpensive portable version and a pack of bamboo skewers from a grocery shop.

© RICK NEVES / SHUTTERSTOCK

All-you-can-eat travel

There's something to be said for the bottomless buffet. Fill up at lunch and you can go all day and get by with a snack for dinner. Try these top buffet tips.

BIG BREAKFASTS

A hotel breakfast will always cost more than a pastry and coffee in the street, even if it's factored into the price of your hotel room, but it makes it easy to fill up for the day and not feel hungry until supper. Bring a press-seal bag or a Tupperware and stow some pastries and fruit in your bag (discreetly, as hotels frown on this) for a mid-morning top up.

THE LUNCH BUFFET

Whether a lunch buffet is good value or not depends on how much you can eat. Buffet lunches included in your room-rate usually cost less than the rate for walk-ins, but you'll still pay more than for a single-course restaurant lunch. Note that spices and flavours can be tuned down, and food is often lukewarm and over-stewed. If the tray is almost empty, hover until staff come with a refill.

GO ALL-INCLUSIVE

Getting all your meals bundled in with your room sounds like a bargain, but you may be trading the freedom of eating where you like for three (unexciting) buffet meals a day. Always check if à-la-carte dining is included. Consider plans like half-board (breakfast and either lunch or dinner) or 'Continental Plan' (room plus breakfast), so you don't miss out on more rewarding food elsewhere.

ALTERNATIVE ALL-YOU-CAN-EATING

Hotels aren't the only places serving bottomless meals. In Asia, look out for lunchtime 'rice plate' dishes, such as the Indian thali – a platter of sauces, rice (or chapatis) and sides. You'll get whichever dishes the cooks are making that day, but there may be free top-ups. In South America, track down the *churrascaria* or *rodízio* – a carnivore's dream of all-you-can-eat meats.

FISH, FIND OR FORAGE

Nature is the world's biggest free grocery store, if you know what to pick and where to pick it. Try these tips for foraging your way around the world.

Berry season
Wild berries and fruit are a feast for free, but you need to know what you're picking. In Nordic countries in late summer, seek out red lingonberries, wild raspberries, blueberry-like bilberries and crowberries and rare, delicious cloudberries (in Sweden, freedom to forage is a legally protected right). Sign up for a wild food course with a local expert so you can identify safe-to-eat species. In the tropics, seek local delicacies, such as wild passionfruit, noni fruit and guavas.

Find a fungus
You need to be careful with fungi, as there are some deadly poisonous species, but if you know your field mushrooms from your fly agaric, the world is a hypermart of free fungi. Woodlands offer particularly rich pickings, but always buy a local mushroom guidebook so you know the species to avoid. With their spongy gills, ceps (*boletus*) are easy to identify, and the inedible species either have a red colour to the flesh, or stain blue when cut. Sign up for a mushroom foraging course for added peace of mind.

Go fish!
You often need a licence to go fishing in rivers and lakes, but fishing in the sea is usually open to all (except from some piers and jetties). If you haven't got room for a rod, pack a weighted hand-reel, which you can use for fishing off rocks or the beach. Grab an anglers' fish identification book so you can spot the species to avoid – some fish have poisonous spines, and members of the pufferfish family have toxic flesh. Ask local fishers for their tips on the best bait (this is often easy-to-find shore shellfish).

Gather shellfish
Again, you need to know the right species, when to harvest them and how to prepare them, but it isn't hard to identify commonly eaten species such as mussels, periwinkles, cockles and clams. Rocky shorelines offer rich pickings, as do sandy beaches at low tide (spot sand-burrowing shells by the shapes they leave at the surface of the sand). Don't overlook crustaceans – prawns are easily caught with a net in the shallows.

STREET FOOD TIPS

Every good traveller knows that the best eats are on the street. Here are our tips for finding a moveable feast.

"People don't tend to queue for worthless food, so if there's a wait to get your hands on it, it's probably going to be great. Other great resources for tips include taxi and Uber drivers, FedEx delivery drivers and anyone else who tends to eat on the go."

Kevin Raub, journalist and Italy expert

1 BREAKFAST ON THE STREETS

Transport hubs are good places to find the first meal of the day. Stalls selling tea and coffee usually offer pastries and bread-like snacks such as China's *youtiao* (fried dough), South Asian *parathas* (flatbreads) or Colombian *arepas* (breakfast sandwiches).

2 OFFICE SNACKS IN THE CBD

Head to the office district at lunchtime on weekdays to find abundant street food at agreeable prices. Look for clusters of food stalls in side alleys and under the arches of elevated overland train lines in between the office buildings.

3 HIT THE MARKET

Markets usually have a cluster of food stalls, serving meals at bargain prices. Come in the morning to enjoy food at its freshest. Souvenir markets often have accompanying food stalls, from Helsinki's Kauppatori to Chiang Mai's 'walking street' markets.

4 NIGHT-MARKET MAGIC

Across Southeast Asia, night markets pop up every evening. Visit those close to transport hubs or along riverbanks and beachfront promenades. Stalls set up from about 5pm and stay open until late, but many markets have one closed day per week.

5 GRAZE THE HAWKER COURTS

The hawker court revolution began in Asia, but specific spaces for food stalls are popping up everywhere. The Asian version is still the best; you'll find courts every few blocks in cities such as Singapore and George Town in Penang. Ask locals for recommendations.

6 FOOD TRUCKS

In developed countries, food trucks set up around popular tourist quarters or in dedicated food-truck parks. Find them using apps such as Roaming Hunger (roaminghunger.com) and StreetFoodFinder (streetfoodfinder.com).

Find the hot spots

Part of the fun of visiting a new place is finding your own favourite food spots, but it never hurts to know what the locals think. Here's how to tap into their dining know-how.

Ask!

If in doubt, ask a local. That could be the receptionist at the hotel, the barista at the neighbourhood coffee shop or the bartender at the pub on the corner. Let them know what you're looking for – cheap and cheerful, authentic and local, swanky and romantic? At smart hotels, the concierge may help you nab a table at the best restaurants in town.

Read the papers

Most large cities have a local newspaper with a dining section (often at the weekend). Some papers – such as Kolkata's *Telegraph*, Melbourne's *The Age*

and London's *Evening Standard* – sponsor annual food awards for the top dining places in town, often accompanied by a special dining guidebook.

Check out listings mags

Look out for listings magazines reviewing the local hot spots. Time Out (timeout.com) has online listings for cities worldwide. Freebie listings magazines in tourist offices, hotel lobbies and cafes are often packed with adverts, but the reviews in the editorial sections can steer you towards good places to graze.

Find the 'destination' restaurants

You'll need advance bookings for many of the world's top-tier restaurants, but first you need to know which restaurants are drawing the plaudits. Start by browsing the Michelin guide (guide.michelin.com) – some single-starred restaurants

are surprisingly affordable – and check the annual lists compiled by World's 50 Best (theworlds50best.com).

Turn to bloggers

Look for city-specific blogs devoted to food, such as New York's Grub Street (grubstreet. com), David Lebovitz in Paris (davidlebovitz.com/paris) and Lorraine Elliott in Sydney (notquitenigella.com). Food blogs tend to be written by genuine foodies, so take a look to see which restaurants are currently getting the love.

Top tip

"When looking for spots to eat in a new place, let your eyes and feet guide you. To kick off the search, I ask my friends or hotel for their recommendation of the best area to explore. Then once I'm there, I'll find the spot with the longest queue or the most people."
Melissa Hie, foodie traveller and founder of girleatworld.net

Low-cost nights out

Going out on the town can cost big bucks, but there's more to nightlife than bars and clubs. Here are some hacks for a less penury-inducing night out.

Go people-watching

People-watching is a great low-cost way to spend an evening. Look for cafes, restaurants or bars with pavement seating facing the hubbub, and settle in to spectate. Alternatively, plenty of countries enjoy an early evening walk, from Mumbai's beachfront promenades to the *passeggiata* that draws thousands of people into the streets nightly in towns all over Italy.

Free culture

There's free culture almost everywhere if you know where to look, from summertime concerts and movie screenings in public parks to bands in neighbourhood pubs. Pick up local listings magazines or ask at the tourist office for the lowdown on free local events. It's also worth checking what's on at international cultural centres, via the likes of the British Council (britishcouncil.org) or Goethe Institute (goethe.de).

Drink with dinner

Drinks often cost less at restaurants, and in some countries the snacks come free with the drinks. In Spain, look for bars serving *pintxos* – bite-sized snacks for a few euros a plate – particularly in the north and the Basque country. In Italy, the tradition manifests itself in the form of aperitivo – order a drink between 7pm and 9pm and nibbles come gratis.

Happy hours

Alcohol can rack up your travel expenses, so make full use of happy hour specials, typically between 5pm and 7pm. Expect drink promotions, two-for-one deals, and sometimes free snacks, but check the terms, as discounts normally cover just the cheaper house drinks.

Have a night in

Takeouts are the key to a cheap night in. Many hotels have common areas, gardens, balconies, terraces or rooftops where you can sit out with some convenience-store beers or a bottle of vino. Check the local rules for public drinking – if it's permitted (or not openly prohibited), parks and beaches are great spots to share drinks with friends.

"In many parts of the world, restaurants are cheaper places to drink than bars, so long as you stick to beers or local wines and spirits. Alternatively, look for BYO restaurants where you can bring your own shop-bought drinks for a nominal corkage charge."

Joe Bindloss,
travel writer

© ANTON GVOZDIKOV / SHUTTERSTOCK

A CHEAP DATE

It can be tricky keeping romance in the air when you're sharing a tent with your socks. Here are some hacks for injecting a little spark when you travel.

★ Share a bottle of wine

With a bottle opener in your bag, anywhere can be the setting for a romantic moment. Buy a bottle of wine and some disposable cups, and take a blanket down to the beach, the nearest park or the hotel rooftop at sunset. Bingo – instant romance, and you might get some bonus stargazing.

★ Take a romantic walk

You'll remember a romantic walk beside the Seine every bit as much as a Michelin-starred meal. Make an occasion of it – pick a location close to water or somewhere high up overlooking the city, and set off in the late afternoon so you can watch the light change over the view.

★ A special table

Plenty of swanky resorts make a feature of exclusive tables for couples laid out on the sand, but you don't need to pay top dollar for a romantic dinner. In seaside locations, many budget cafes lay out tables on the beach (Bali's Jimbaran Beach deserves a special mention), where you can sup while wafted by sea breezes.

★ Movie night

Many cities lay on free (or cheap) open-air movie screenings in public parks in the summer; the choice of movies can be hit or miss, but you can't fault the setting. Alternatively, stream a suitably romantic movie on your laptop (or grab something from a local DVD store).

★ Fetch something special for your significant other

Romance is often about little gestures. Get up before your partner and nip to the market for fresh tropical fruit or a superior-quality espresso and a *pain au chocolate*. If it's later in the day, make an excuse to leave the hotel and come back with ice cream.

TAKING CARE OF THE PRACTICALITIES

Travel money tips

Money makes the world go round, so keeping your cash safe is a key concern when you travel. Mix up your options – smart travellers never rely wholly on either plastic or cash. Here are our top tips.

★ Carrying cash

Hard currency has its advantages – for one thing, you'll almost always be able to find someone who can exchange a few bills, even if it's a local shopkeeper. On the other hand, cash can't be replaced if it gets stolen, so always make a detailed plan for keeping your money safe – see p116. Investigate which currency is the most useful to carry; some destinations have a preference for US dollars or euros, but you'll rarely have trouble changing British pounds, Australian, New Zealand and Canadian dollars and Japanese yen.

★ Go with cheques?

While they are famously easy to cancel and replace if they get lost or stolen, travellers cheques are falling from favour. They're still useful in destinations such as the US and Europe, but check the best currency to carry (usually, it's US dollars or euros). Bring cheques in larger denominations to avoid paying commission charges every time you change 20 bucks. Check if banks or forex exchange offices give better rates, and make a habit of using places that don't charge a commission. And keep a record of the cheque numbers and the issuer's emergency contact number somewhere separate from the actual cheques in case you need to report a theft or loss and request replacements.

★ Use a debit card

Debit cards have the advantage of being they're linked to your bank account, so it's harder to spend money you don't have. On the flip side, if your account is compromised, you could lose a lot more – unless you promptly cancel your card. As a precaution, you may want to keep just a small amount in the account linked to the card, moving the rest of your funds to a separate account. Many travellers use debit cards only for ATM withdrawals to reduce the risk of being scammed by shopkeepers. Note that most ATM withdrawals incur charges – sometimes from both your home bank and the issuing bank, so make fewer withdrawals for larger amounts to keep a lid on costs.

★ Go prepaid

Prepaid cards are a neat solution to the travel card conundrum. You can load up the card with value in either your home currency or the destination currency, and use it to pay like you would with a debit card. Do some research on the fees levied – there may be charges for every transaction, particularly if there's a change of currency. The prepaid card from Revolut (revolut.com) doesn't charge for conversions on weekdays, but ATM withdrawals incur a fee above a fixed threshold per month. Other popular cards include Wise (wise.com), EasyFX (easyfx.com) and Starling Bank (starlingbank.com), which offers a superior travel money card with no fees for ATMs and most transactions, linked to its online bank account.

★ Do it on credit

So long as you pay off the balance every month, a credit card is a great travel tool. You can pay anywhere electronic payment is accepted, you can cancel the card if it's stolen, you have a reserve of emergency cash, you can rack up points for flights and hotels, and you often get insurance for purchases. Shop around for the best deals – comparison sites such as Money Supermarket (moneysupermarket.com) and the Points Guy (thepointsguy.com) can help – and keep an eye on the APR (annual percentage rate) as well as the points, bonuses and perks. Visa and Mastercard are accepted almost everywhere; Amex, JCB and Diners Club less so – don't rely on them as your sole payment option.

Digital money

Payment apps are the new way to pay, but watch for new tech scams. Follow this advice when paying by device.

Paying by phone

Paying via smartphone apps is certainly convenient, but it does mean flashing a highly stealable device in public every time you pay – always scope out your surroundings before whipping out your iPhone 14. Check which apps locals are using and follow their lead. Apple Pay and Google Pay are the big international players, but there are loads of local mobile payment apps, from Africa's M-Pesa (see vodafone. com) to China's Alipay (global. alipay.com) and WeChat (wechat.com).

Use PayPal

For many sights, tours, hotels and transport, you can book online using PayPal, and its buyer protection policies will give you some recourse in the event of a dispute. PayPal keeps your payment details hidden, but if someone has your password, they can still access your account, so don't log on from public computers or unsecured networks and turn on two-factor authentication, requiring a code sent to your phone to log in.

Money by wire

Western Union (westernunion. com) and MoneyGram (moneygram.com) offices can be used to transfer or receive money almost anywhere, but exchange rates can be poor, and the fees and charges can mount up. Reserve wire services for making payments in off-grid destinations and for transferring money to yourself in an emergency.

DIGITAL PAYMENT SECURITY TIPS

Always activate your phone's security measures, particularly the auto-lock function and biometric security, and keep a hard-copy record of your bank's card-cancellation number somewhere separate from your phone. Also switch on payment notifications on your banking app so you can spot if someone else is using your account. Consider turning off Near Field Communication (NFC) and Wi-Fi on your phone when you aren't using it to keep your accounts safe, and keep the Find My Phone app active, so you can remotely inactivate your phone if it goes missing.

CARD SMARTS

Credit and debit cards are a low-stress way to access your money overseas, but they come with their own risks. Try these top card tips.

"Relying on bank or credit cards can be a gamble in countries with unreliable electricity supplies. I once had a card eaten by an ATM in Nepal after the power failed while I was making a withdrawal. Where possible, stick to ATMs inside the bank during opening hours."

Joe Bindloss,
travel writer

 ## KNOW HOW YOUR CARD WORKS

Call your bank to check if there's a foreign transaction fee for using ATMs from other networks, or fees for making payments in a different currency. If there are charges, you may be able to find a card with lower costs. The Points Guy (thepointsguy.com) has tips.

 ## ATM SAFETY

ATMs are prime targets for thieves. To stay safe, keep your PIN number hidden and use ATMs inside banks or shopping malls with security on the door (or a private booth) when possible. Examine the ATM to make sure it hasn't been rigged to skim card details.

 ## CARRY A CURVE

Consider using a Curve card (curve.com) – you can link all your debit and credit cards to this one handy bit of plastic and make transactions and ATM withdrawals from your accounts just using the Curve card, at favourable rates.

 ## DON'T GET CLONED

Always check that card payment devices haven't been tampered with, and guard your PIN. Using contactless payment can be less risky. Carry a Radio Frequency Identification blocker, such as the card guard from GoTravel (go.travel) to protect the card's smart chip.

 ## USE THE RIGHT ATMS

Research the best ATMs to use; they don't all take foreign cards and charges vary. Carry the right cards – Visa and Mastercard are safe bets. Avoid ATMs that charge a fixed 'withdrawal fee', and make fewer withdrawals, of larger amounts, to minimise charges.

 ## CARD CANCELLING

If your precious card goes walkabout, cancel it (or lock it with your phone banking app) as soon as you notice it's gone. Stay cancel-ready by keeping the cancellation phone number somewhere safe, separate from your cards.

Foreign exchange for beginners

If you're carrying cash, investigate how the local foreign-exchange market works. Being prepared will help you make your money go further.

Compare rates

Change money in the destination to get a better rate than you would back home. Forex booths often compete over rates to attract customers, so shop around. Rates offered at the airport are usually lower than rates in town, so change just enough to get into the city. Always check whether the office charges a commission – banks often levy lower charges than private forex desks.

Get the right bills

Do some research into the best currency and denominations to carry. US dollars, UK pounds and euros are accepted almost everywhere, but some places offer better rates for bigger bills. Check the condition of your banknotes – only pristine, undamaged bills may be accepted – and get some of your local currency in smaller bills, so you have some petty cash for small transactions. Carefully count your cash; legitimate mistakes happen, but dodgy operators may try to shortchange you.

The black market

In some countries, the black market offers much better rates than official forex services, so discreetly ask if shops and accommodation staff are willing to exchange at preferential rates. Never exchange money with shady characters who accost you in the street – the risks of being scammed or robbed are huge.

Can't find a forex desk?

Hotels will often exchange cash (and sometimes travellers cheques), though often at disadvantageous rates. Many tourist shops accept payment in foreign currency, which can be a better deal than changing money and paying transaction fees or a commission.

Leftover currency

Try not to leave your destination with too much local currency – it may be hard to exchange back home. If you take your receipt back to the place you exchanged in the first place, they may buy back your leftovers without commission. Only change at the airport if you have to – rates can be insulting.

Top tip

"Try not to get stuck with a ripped, scribbled-on or otherwise damaged bill. Even though it's technically still legal tender, you may have a nightmare of a time getting anyone to accept it. When you change money, always check every bill over before you leave the exchange desk to catch any duds."
Joe Bindloss, travel writer

ESSENTIAL MONEY APPS

Having a smartphone in your pocket is like bringing your own financial expert along on the road. With a roaming package or local data SIM, you can check the latest exchange rates, compare prices and safely look in on your accounts. Here are some essential apps to load before you travel.

Your banking app

Use the mobile banking app from your home bank to log into your accounts, check balances and arrange payments without having to enter sensitive information over an insecure internet connection.

XE
(xe.com)

This trusted currency-exchange app offers real-time exchange rates for pretty much every global currency, and it stores the last-checked rates for your 10 favourite currencies for times when you can't get online.

Tripcoin
(tripcoinapp.com)

A free, user-friendly iPhone budgeting app with built-in currency converter and integrated backups via Dropbox.

WeSwap
(weswap.com)

Combining an app and a prepaid card, WeSwap uses peer-to-peer transfers to cut out the cost of foreign exchange in 18 currencies, but you'll need to wait seven days to access your money (or pay a fee).

Local mobile payment apps

Many countries have their own apps for phone payments as an alternative to Apple Pay or Google Pay, from Africa's Orange Money to India's Paytm. Ask locals about the most secure and accepted apps.

Trabee Pocket
(trabeepocket.com)

A handy expenses tracker that can help you keep on top of your travel costs. Set a trip budget and split your costs into different categories – handy for spotting whether your beer bill is pushing you over the limit.

Splittr
(splittr.io)

A neat tool for sharing costs and splitting bills if you're travelling in a group, as well as monitoring your own travel costs.

Starling
(starlingbank.com)

Part bank account, part prepaid debit card, this digital bank charges no fees for overseas ATM withdrawals and card transactions made with its contactless Mastercard (which also works via mobile payment apps).

Keeping your money safe

Your travel money keeps you on the move, so keep it safe. Carrying cash comes with risks, but no form of travel money is completely secure, so always bring several ways to pay. Here are some top hacks.

Be smart with cash

You'll want some of your travel funds in cash, just in case, but don't keep all your bucks in one basket. Store an emergency stash somewhere that thieves won't expect to find it – in an old lip-balm tube in your washbag for example – and divide the remainder into a small amount of 'petty cash' and a larger 'bank' that you only open in private.

Wallet wisdom

If you must use a wallet, carry only what you need for the day and keep it out of sight. A wallet-sized bulge in your back trouser pocket is like a neon sign saying, 'pick my pocket'. Open jacket pockets are only marginally better – stick to zip-up pockets or your hard-to-access front trouser pockets.

Wallet alternatives

Use a money belt or hidden money pouch as an alternative to a wallet. Both sit next to your skin, so you can feel them being interfered with. However, muggers are smart enough to know they exist – having a mostly empty wallet that you can hand over after a token protest isn't a bad decoy measure.

Be ATM wise

Outdoor ATMs are popular targets for thieves so, where possible, use the machines inside the bank or at shopping centres with security guards. Don't make ATMs your only option – some machines only accept local cards, and a power cut or network error could put your cash out of reach.

Use the hotel safe

Don't assume your hotel room is 100% secure. Keep your money in the hotel safe when you go out or hide it somewhere unexpected – tucked inside your socks or shoes is less obvious than pushed under the mattress.

© MICHAEL O'KEENE / SHUTTERSTOCK

UNEXPECTED COSTS TO WATCH OUT FOR

Travel can be a minefield of hidden extras and covert costs. Here are some financial tripwires to be aware of.

Sales taxes

Always check the sales tax. In countries that don't include taxes in the marked prices, such as the US, VAT can add as much as 20% to your bills. Hotels often quote prices without tax, using the suffix '++', meaning 'plus sales tax and service charge', so ask reception to give you the all-in price. If pay VAT on a luxury purchase, check if you can claim back the tax at the airport when you leave (you'll usually need a special receipt from the shop).

Automatic service charges

Every country has its own rules, but some hotels and restaurants automatically add a service charge to your bill, even if staff don't do anything obvious to earn it. Watch for controversial 'resort fees' for beach resort stays in the US. If you spot such a charge on your bill, ask if it's discretionary, and only pay if you feel the service warrants a reward.

Tourist taxes

Destinations around the world are tackling overtourism with tourist taxes, usually tagged onto hotel room rates. Venice levies a €3 to €10 per day tourist tax for overnight stays, while Thailand is planning to introduce a 150–300 baht tax for tourists in 2023, payable on arrival. You can't avoid these taxes, so set aside a kitty for the extra cost.

DON'T FORGET TO TIP

Japan, China and South Korea don't have a tradition of tipping, and many other countries let you tip as you see fit, but skip the tip in the US and you risk being chased down the street! Ask a local for advice on local tipping etiquette, including the right percentage to leave (remember, staff may depend on tips for their living). You may need to tip restaurant staff, hotel staff, taxi drivers, tour guides and support staff if you go trekking, so budget a little extra to cover this often-overlooked cost.

Managing money emergencies

OK, your worst travel nightmare has happened – you've lost your wallet. What now? Follow these vital steps...

Protect your digital funds

As soon as you realise your wallet or purse has gone walkabout, call the bank and cancel your credit and debit cards. If you still have your mobile phone, your home banking app may let you apply a temporary lock on your cards to buy you time to make sure your cards really are lost. Thankfully, you were smart and kept your bank's emergency phone number separate from your cards.

Get a police report

There is little chance of the police getting back your money if it's stolen. That's about the same likelihood as your insurance company replacing your money without a police report. If your wallet is lost or stolen, go straight to the police, file a report and keep a copy, so you can make an insurance claim if you need to.

Getting replacement cards & cheques

If you're on a long trip, your bank may be able to send replacement cards or travellers cheques to you overseas, but there'll be a charge, it takes time and it may not be possible outside the capital city. To avoid this complicated situation, carry a backup card somewhere separate from your main stash so you aren't left without options.

Phone a friend

If you're genuinely stuck without funds, call someone back home – if necessary, via free video-calling software on your phone or laptop – and ask if they can arrange a money transfer. Western Union (westernunion. com) and MoneyGram (moneygram.com) have offices worldwide where you can pick up the funds.

Be ready to abort

Losing your wallet or passport might mean the end of your trip – unless you can support yourself for long enough for replacements to arrive. If not, contact your embassy to explain the situation. They may be willing to repatriate you, but you'll have to pay back the costs.

© SKT STUDIO / SHUTTERSTOCK

LEARNING THE LANGUAGE

"Memorise a sentence that will explain your non-native-speaker status and put you more at ease. Starting an exchange with something like, 'I'm trying to learn [language] and I need practice, please excuse all my mistakes!' will put the listener in an understanding frame of mind and make you feel less mortified by your inevitable boo-boos."

Janine Eberle,
translator, Paris

Not everyone is a natural-born polyglot, but with a few apps and hacks you should be able to pick up enough words to get by.

★ Learn the basics

Lonely Planet publishes a full range of pocket-sized phrasebooks, but phone apps such as Duolingo (duolingo.com), Memrise (memrise.com) and Babbel (uk.babbel.com) let you hear what a language should sound like. For practice with free-form conversations, consider Hellotalk (hellotalk.com) – a social network that pairs speakers of different languages.

★ Use pictures

Being unable to speak the language doesn't mean you can't communicate. Tuck a pad and pen into your daypack and you can draw what you need, Pictionary-style. For complex languages with their own scripts, consider carrying a visual dictionary, such as *Point It* by Dieter Gräf, or Dorling Kindersley's *Pocket Visual Dictionary*.

★ Write it down

To find addresses overseas, ask a local to write the details down in the local script so you can show this to taxi drivers and people you ask for directions. Always grab the hotel card from reception – if you get lost, show it to a taxi driver and they'll whisk you back.

★ Practise!

Use the local language as much as possible – conversations with real people are the best way to learn. To start the ball rolling, equip yourself with a basic armoury of key phrases – hello, goodbye, how much, numbers, and basics for finding a hotel room, ordering a meal and navigating transport – and keep these handy for quick reference.

★ How to cheat

Google Translate (translate.google.com) is invaluable for drafting emails to hotels and tour operators. Keep the app handy on your phone for in-person conversations, and for translating signs and menus using your phone camera. Other translation apps include Microsoft Translator (translator.microsoft.com), DeepL Translate (deepl.com), iTranslate (itranslate.com), and SayHi (sayhi.com), which can translate spoken words in real time.

GETTING CONNECTED

Going online while you travel opens up a new front in the battle against cybercrime. Here's how to protect your valuable data on the road.

"Travelling with just a smartphone is a great way to go, as you can avoid bringing a laptop or using unknown devices in places like hotels or internet cafes. Just make sure it is backed up properly, for example with iCloud, which will enable you to remotely wipe it should it be stolen, and restore all your personal information on a new device.'

Doug Rimington, photographer and IT expert (@detunephotography)

 ## PUBLIC COMPUTER CAUTION

Only use public computers if you have no choice; you don't know what software is running and staff rarely keep on top of security updates. Use 'incognito' or 'private' browsing, log out of any sites, clear the browser cache and reboot before you leave.

 ## MOBILE HACKS

To improve security, turn off Wi-Fi and Bluetooth whenever you're not using them, or flip on Airplane mode. Also turn off Wi-Fi Assist and Auto-Updates – both will wick away your mobile data without you being aware of it.

 ## GET A DATA SIM

With an unlocked phone and a data SIM package from a local phone company, you'll get the cheapest data and reliable connections. Look for mobile phone desks offering tourist SIM packages at the airport – sometimes the SIM is free, so you just pay for data.

 ## SAFE SURFING

Never enter vulnerable data, such as your credit card number, over a public Wi-Fi network. Cellular data is harder to intercept, so use your smartphone (Wi-Fi off) for online banking. Before you leave home, set up two-factor authentication for all your accounts.

 ## DATA-ROAMING PITFALLS

Unless there's a reciprocal deal with your home country, data roaming charges can sting. Buy a data package from your home provider to lock in fixed gigabytes at a capped rate, or turn off data roaming – texting doesn't count and you can get online via Wi-Fi.

 ## VPNS

Virtual Private Networks secure your device. Nord VPN (nordvpn.com) and Express VPN (expressvpn.com) are solid. Tunnelbear (tunnelbear.com) and Windscribe (windscribe.com) have cheap starter packs; or try Google's one.google.com/about/vpn.

Be document smart

Your travel documents are vital, and you always need to be able to access them, even during a power cut or a tropical storm. Try these hacks to keep your paperwork safe.

Take copies

Carry photocopies of every important document – your passport ID pages and visa, your driving licence, the contact details of your embassy, the numbers for cancelling your bank cards, the claims numbers for your insurance company, your transport tickets, and anything else that you might need to call on during your travels. Store these copies in a waterproof, sealable plastic bag, and keep them as safe as you would if they were originals.

Bring digital copies

Paper gets torn, and photocopy ink gets worn, so carry a digital backup of your documents. Take scans or snap photos with your phone and email them to yourself so you can get to them in several different ways. Email copies to people back home too, so you can call a friend if you lose everything.

E-ticket tips

If you're relying on e-tickets, print backup copies and ensure you have a way to charge your digital devices – you don't want to run out of power just as you reach the terminal. Always read the small print for any e-tickets, as you may need to check-in online, with steep fees for completing the whole process at the terminal.

Take care of originals

Most documents can be reprinted, but replacing your passport or driving licence is a major headache, so keep them secure – in a hidden pouch on your person or locked in the hotel safe. If you rent a vehicle, be wary of leaving your passport as the deposit – ask if you can leave cash or pay with a credit card instead.

DEVICES YOU NEED

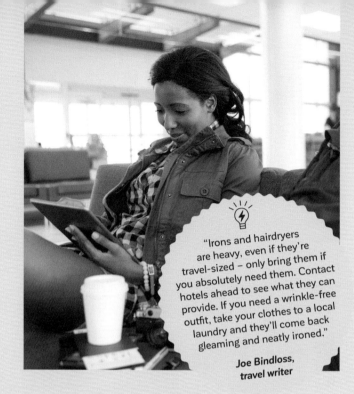

Don't go overboard with devices – travel isn't about doing the same things you do at home. Along with something to record your travels (see p33), here's the core tech to consider.

> "Irons and hairdryers are heavy, even if they're travel-sized – only bring them if you absolutely need them. Contact hotels ahead to see what they can provide. If you need a wrinkle-free outfit, take your clothes to a local laundry and they'll come back gleaming and neatly ironed."
>
> **Joe Bindloss,**
> **travel writer**

★ Your laptop or tablet

A lightweight laptop or tablet is a genuinely useful piece of travel kit. You can check emails and do online banking in privacy, you can back up your travel photos, and you have a portable digital entertainment centre for long journeys and listless evenings in transit towns. Consider buying a neoprene case to protect it from accidental knocks, and look online to see if you can find a lightweight charger. Carry an external hard drive too, so you can also back up your laptop.

★ Your smartphone

With a decent smartphone, you might be able to skip the laptop or iPad. Load it up with essential apps (see p35 and p115), turn on two-stage security and carry an external power bank to keep it charged. Make sure it's not locked to your home network so you can use a local SIM. Some travellers prefer to bring a cheap, low-tech phone for calls and texting

to reduce the risk of getting robbed of their Apple-made pride and joy.

★ A music player & headphones

It's not just music to keep you entertained on long bus rides, it's portable privacy. Forget legacy tech – a digital music player is the smart option. You could always put your music on your phone, but that means having one of your most valuable possessions on display; playing your tunes on a cheap MP3 player is less risky.

★ Power adaptors

You'll need something to fit your chargers into the local sockets, so always check the local socket configurations and bring an adaptor. Some hotel rooms have only a lone socket, powering the bedside light or the TV, so rather than carrying multiple adaptors, bring one with multiple USB ports, or a multiplug power strip from home.

Protect your tech

Your phone, laptop and camera are your windows to the world, so keep them safe. Here are some hacks for protecting precious tech.

Get insured

Travel insurance isn't always generous when it comes to payouts for your expensive electronics. Always check the small print, noting the excess and the maximum payment for any individual items; if you're travelling with a Leica or a Rolex, you may need to add it to the policy as a named risk (for an extra charge). To reduce the chance of theft or damage, keep your precious tech safely packed away when you aren't using it.

Be bag-snatch smart

Electronics are a favourite target for opportunistic theft, so never leave your valuable tech on public display. Pavement cafes are prime locations for grab-and-run crimes – don't leave your phone or laptop unsupervised on the table. If you put your bag down, keep it under the table in front of you, not on the back of the chair – and put one chair leg over the strap so it can't subtly be removed.

Don't flash your phone

Thieves on bikes and mopeds do a lively business in phones snatched from the hands of travellers who walk along the street making phone calls. Call from your hotel instead – it's quieter and safer – and keep your phone tucked away in a zipped inside pocket or hidden pouch in your clothes when it's not in use. If you check your coat at a restaurant or bar, never leave any devices in the pockets – mobile devices are famously, well, mobile.

Secure your devices

Always turn on the security options on your phone and laptop, and use two-factor authentication whenever possible. It could be the difference between losing your phone, and losing all the money in your bank account to identity theft. Also turn on two-factor authentication for online communications and financial websites so you get a phone alert if someone tries to access your money or messages.

Staying on the right side of the law

Ignorance is no excuse in the eyes of the law, so make sure you have a basic knowledge of local laws that might affect travellers, particularly when crossing borders. Try these law-abiding tips.

Drugs

Some countries impose jail terms for the possession of even small amounts of controlled drugs, and many destinations in Asia impose the death penalty for drug smuggling. By far the best policy is to stay away from drugs, unless they are legal or decriminalised. Even a minor conviction for possession of marijuana can make it harder to get visas in future, so save your rolling papers for destinations where cannabis is legal, such as California or Canada.

Import restrictions

Importing controlled substances, explosives and endangered species is banned for obvious reasons, but lots of countries also ban the import of vaping devices, including Cambodia and Singapore. Australia and New Zealand have strict rules on the import of fruit, vegetables and other items that could harbour foreign pests – check the regs at abf.gov.au and customs.govt.nz. Japan bans the import of some over-the-counter and prescription medicines – check the rules at www.mhlw.go.jp.

Road rules

Travellers often fall foul of local traffic laws – usually by speeding, parking in the wrong places, or going the wrong way up one-way roads. If you drive, read up on the local road rules (including helmet requirements for motorcycles) and diligently obey road signs. If you get a legitimate traffic fine, pay it promptly – you don't want an unpaid fine hanging over you the next time you try to enter the country.

Bribes

If you get asked for a bribe, you're in a tricky position. Paying up is usually illegal, but not paying can get you into more trouble. If the 'gratuity' isn't too much, it's likely to be a routine sting, and paying up can make the problem go away, but it's better to avoid putting yourself in a vulnerable position in the first place by diligently following local laws.

Be a considerate traveller

Remember that you're a guest in someone else's country, so avoid causing offence by respecting the house rules.

Taboo topics

It's rarely a good idea to criticise religion, the government or the royal family of whatever country you're travelling through. In Thailand, lèse-majesté – speaking ill of the king or royal family – can earn you a jail term. Getting involved in conversations with locals about controversial topics can also get them into trouble; save the political debates for friends in your hotel room.

Respect religion

You don't have to sign up for salvation, but respect local religious traditions. If a temple says no footwear, take off your shoes. If a mosque says cover your hair, legs and shoulders, pop on a headscarf and wrap around a sarong. In Buddhist countries, avoid pointing your feet towards a Buddha image and respect Buddhist imagery – people have been deported from Sri Lanka for sporting Buddha tattoos and T-shirts.

Bathing rules

Countries that love public bathing, such as Japan and Iceland, often have strict codes of conduct when it comes to cleanliness. Always wash thoroughly before getting into the water – the showers are there for a reason. Note that some countries require tight, Speedo-style swimsuits for the pool; wear board shorts and you may be turned away at the poolside.

Greet like a local

If there's a local tradition of shaking hands, you'll be OK thrusting out a paw. If not, follow the lead of locals – physical contact between men and women who don't know each other is frowned on in many countries.

Be a responsible snapper

Ask before taking pictures – it's only polite. Some religious sites are off limits, and some tribal people object to being, well, objectified by snappers. Photography is also unwise around demonstrations and protests, military or political sites, major transport hubs and anywhere near border crossings.

TIPS FOR WOMEN TRAVELLERS

The world has a way to go before female travellers can enjoy the same easy experience of travel as the gents. Try these hacks for women on the road.

"Do some research before you travel about what to wear. Before I left for my first trip to India in 2005, I read that it's a good idea for women travellers to wear Indian clothes, such as the three-piece salwar kameez. I took this advice to heart, and it seemed to garner respect from the local people wherever I went."

Mariellen Ward, travel blogger and founder of India for Beginners (indiaforbeginners.com)

Beachwear

Again, let local women be your guide. In some countries, beachwear is only for the beach, so bring a sarong if you plan to walk around. Where women swim fully clothed, popping a T-shirt and long shorts over your suit can help.

Religious sensibilities

Religions can be a bit behind-the-times when it comes to gender equality. If you plan to visit religious buildings, you'll need to be ready to follow the rules, whether that means entering through the door reserved for women or covering your hair on entry (always carry a scarf in your day bag).

Follow the lead of local women

Some countries have strongly conservative attitudes, particularly when it comes to women's attire. For an easier trip, follow the lead of local women when it comes to dress. Often this means covering your legs and shoulders and avoiding daring necklines and exposed midriffs. The South Asian salwar kameez – a long shirt with loose-fitting trousers – is a great outfit for tropical travel, even outside Asia.

Avoiding unwanted attention

Female travellers use all sorts of tricks to avoid unsolicited male attention. The fake wedding ring is a favourite, as is referring to 'my husband' (even if he doesn't actually exist). Don't start idle conversations with men as these might be misinterpreted (sadly, some gents base their opinions of foreign women on Hollywood stereotypes). Wearing dark glasses and headphones can reduce intrusive encounters.

Staying safe

Follow the same safety rules as at home – be careful about walking alone in empty places (particularly after dark), avoid being alone with men you don't know, and watch out for wandering hands, particularly in festival crowds. Don't hitchhike, and never get into a taxi containing another man in addition to the driver.

Watch your drinks

We hate having to say this, but be wary of spiked drinks. Never leave your drink unattended, and politely decline offers of drinks from strangers – buying your own drinks can also put-off bothersome would-be suitors.

Transport tips

Take advantage of women-only spaces on public transport, such as Japan's women-only train carriages and India's all-female Sakha Consulting Wings (sakhaconsultingwings.com) cab company. They may be a sticking plaster for a bigger societal problem, but you'll avoid a lot of hassle.

Take a women-only tour

Plenty of agencies arrange women-only tours and activities. Intrepid (intrepidtravel.com) has a particularly wide range of trips, treks and tours. Also look out for all-women trekking and adventure companies, such as Nepal's 3 Sisters (3sistersadventuretrek.com), Wilderness Scotland (wildernessscotland.com/women-in-adventure) and the US REI Coop (rei.com/adventures/t/womens).

Safety in numbers

Having a travel companion – or three – of any sex or gender can cut down on the hassle significantly. Post requests for female travel companions on travel noticeboards (see p23) or try the all-women app TravelSisters (travelsisters.co).

Health considerations

Check the availability of period products and contraception, and pack treatments for the likes of thrush – common in the tropics. Many women prefer a mooncup to tampons or pads. If you're travelling while pregnant, see your doctor and talk to your airline; some carriers won't fly women in the third trimester.

Local laws

We don't condone it, but many countries have laws that restrict female freedoms, so be aware of the rules and stay on the right side of the law. Take extra care in countries where women are treated differently to men in law, such as the Gulf States, where victims of sexual assault risk being prosecuted under morality laws.

Listen to women

There are some great blogs written by women who travel, for women who travel. Good sites include Adventurous Kate (adventurouskate.com), Breathedreamgo (breathedreamgo.com), Hey Nadine (heynadine.com), Runaway Juno (runawayjuno.com) and World of Wanderlust (worldofwanderlust.com).

SOLO TRAVEL

Solo travel is one of those experiences that starts out challenging but soon becomes liberating. Here are some tricks to help you get the best from the experience.

"The first time you travel by yourself can be daunting, but stick with it. It won't take too many days before you start to love the freedom to do whatever you want, whenever you want, without having to run everything past a committee."

Joe Bindloss,
travel writer

 1 **STAY SOCIALLY**

You won't meet people to chat to if you're stuck in your hotel room. Stay in places with shared spaces and you'll soon connect with other travellers. Lonely Planet's 'top picks' accommodation suggestions normally attract a gregarious crowd.

 2 **BE SOCIABLE**

Being a solo traveller doesn't mean you need to be alone 24/7. Get into the habit of talking to other travellers. Just being friendly will take you a long way, and many travellers are itching to share their experiences and love of travel with someone else.

 3 **DON'T BE AFRAID TO BE ALONE**

The magic of solo travel is that you call the shots. You can see what you want, whenever you want. Even if you tag along with others for a few days, it's fine to head off in another direction if your interests diverge – swap contact details and you may hook up again.

 4 **GATHER A GROUP**

If you go it alone, you'll be stung for the 'single's tax' on rooms and organised tours, and you'll pay the full whack if you charter a vehicle. Reach out to other travellers, or pop messages on noticeboards (or on the web – see p23) to find buddies to split the bill.

 5 **GET USED TO EATING ALONE**

The first time you eat alone can feel strange, but you'll get to finish your dessert without anyone stealing a bite. Bring a book or digital device and run through some emails or social posts if you feel uncomfortable doing nothing while you wait for your meal.

 6 **TAKE A TOUR**

Adventurous tours of the kind offered by Intrepid (intrepidtravel.com), G Adventures (gadventures.com) and Exodus (exodus.com) are a great way to connect with others. Consider joining a group tour for part of the journey for a break from solitude.

7 GO UNDERCOVER

There are times you'll want to be alone. To preserve your personal space, put on sunglasses and pop in headphones, or pull out a book. Women travellers have tricks for discouraging unwanted male attention, such as wearing a fake wedding band – see p126.

9 BE SOLO SAFE

Be cautious about walking alone at night and taking more risky forms of transport, such as hitchhiking or lifts from locals, particularly if you're a solo woman. If you're heading into unpopulated areas, tell someone where you're going and when you plan to be back.

8 KEEP IN TOUCH

Folks back home may worry, so check-in regularly by email, text or via social networks and video-calling and messaging apps such as WhatsApp. Set up a group for your nearest and dearest to let them know you're safe without messaging everyone individually.

10 DON'T TREK ALONE

Trekking solo is never advisable – if you get in trouble, there'll be nobody to go for help. Find other trekkers for company on the trails, or hire a guide and porter for added insights on the communities and environments you're travelling through.

© WILDERNESS SCOTLAND

11 TOP HEALTH TIPS

Nobody likes getting sick, and that goes double when you travel. Try these hacks to stay healthy on the road.

"Pack condoms when travelling – the quality and size range in some countries is poor. Safer sex means using condoms and water-based lubricant from start to finish. Reducing the number of sexual partners significantly reduces your risk. Beware of alcohol and recreational drugs destroying one's enthusiasm for safer sex, and have regular sexual health check-ups: some germs have no symptoms at first."

Dr Deb Mills, health expert and founder of thetraveldoctor.com.au

1 Vaccinations
Always see the doctor at least a month before you go, to check which vaccinations you need for your destination. Many inoculations need to be topped up every five to 10 years. Try your own medical practice first, before going to a pricey travel clinic.

2 Antimalarials
There's no malaria vaccine, but antimalarial drugs can prevent infection. Get them early – you may need to start before you leave. Get the right drugs for your destination as some strains are immune to certain drugs.

3 Avoiding mosquito bites
Mosquitoes carry everything from malaria to Zika fever and dengue. Avoid bites by using a repellent with a high concentration of DEET (diethyltoluamide), particularly on exposed skin, and wear light colours in preference to dark.

4 Sleeping in mosquito country
Mosquitoes are most active at night (and sunrise and sunset), but some species are active in the day. For protection while you sleep, use mosquito nets saturated with permethrin, mosquito coils or plug-in repellent devices.

5 Bigger biters
Sharks and crocodiles aren't usually a risk, but heed local advice on where to swim or surf. Snakes are more common – wear boots, socks and thick trousers when hiking and move slowly. Bites from dogs and cats can transmit rabies – resist the urge to pet them.

6 Avoiding stings
Get local advice on the creepy crawlies to avoid. Be cautious of bees and other stinging insects. Spider bites are rare, but be careful walking through undergrowth or moving rocks and dead wood. The sea is full of things that sting – heed warnings about jellyfish, fish with poisonous spines, and seashells that inject venom (such as Australia's cone shells).

7 Respiratory bugs
It's wise to get vaccinated against COVID-19 and flu. A medical mask is a sensible precaution in crowds and confined spaces (it will also keep out a lot of the atmospheric pollution that can increase vulnerability to coughs and colds).

8 Skin infections

Hot, humid weather raises the risk of fungal infections, such as athlete's foot, jock itch and thrush. Keep your body clean, wear loose-fitting clothing, and carry antifungal treatments. Drink lots of water to reduce the risk of urinary tract infections.

9 Stomach bugs

Basic hygiene will help you avoid most stomach bugs – see p100. Always wash your hands with soap and water (or use an alcohol-based disinfectant gel) before you eat, particularly if you'll be touching food with your hands.

10 Be kind to your gut

Every country has its own biological ecosystem, so help your gut adjust by eating healthily. Boost your intake of fresh fruit and veg (washed in purified water or peeled) and encourage friendly gut bacteria with natural yoghurt.

11 Keep fit

Don't forget to exercise while you travel. Bring a skipping rope, or clothes you can run in, and head to the nearest park or beach; or do resistance exercises such as sit-ups, squats and push-ups. Take advantage of free hotel gyms and go for lots of walks.

PARASITIC CREEPY CRAWLIES

Ticks can carry all sort of nasties, so check your body after walking in undergrowth, and remove with tweezers. In South America, use repellent and treated nets to deter beetles that carry Chagas' disease. Leeches are unpleasant rather than a big disease risk – use salt or slide the mouth parts off with a fingernail, then use antiseptic cream.

Avoiding the scams

Scamming travellers has been an industry since at least the time of 14th-century explorer Ibn Battuta, so be on the lookout for these common scams.

Touts

Touts gather everywhere tourists gather, steering travellers to hotels, restaurants, shops and dodgy travel agents where you'll pay more to cover their commission. Refuse their assistance firmly but politely and find your own way.

The gem scam

If anyone tries to sell you gems, or carpets, or any other pricey items with the promise that you can sell them for a profit at home, you're being taken for a ride. Buy things because you like them, rather than as an investment.

The old switcheroo

If you buy anything to be shipped home or packed for transport, make sure you see your item being packed. Some shopkeepers aren't above swapping your purchase for a cheaper item while your attention is distracted.

The broken meter

Many taxi and rickshaw drivers dislike using the meter like vampires dislike garlic. If you can't persuade the driver to use the meter, either try another cab, or bargain a fare with the driver before you board – ask your hotel for the going rate.

Transport scams

Be wary of travel agencies offering 'international bus' tickets, where you pay extra for a deluxe direct bus, only to find yourself taking multiple ordinary buses to cross the border. Stick to legitimate travel agents – if anyone 'helped' you find the agency without you asking, you're probably being lined up for a scam.

The fake tourist office

Be suspicious of signs saying 'Tourist Office' on the front of tour agencies – only trust information from the official tourist office, which can usually be identified by the fact that staff don't try to sell you anything!

Phoney cops

Watch out for people pretending to be officials. Decline offers to settle 'fines' on the spot – ask to see ID and say you're happy to sort this out at the police station, then the 'problem' may suddenly be resolved.

TIPS FOR HAGGLERS

Haggling is a ballet, not a boxing match. The right amount of give and take will get you what you want at a price that's fair to both parties. Try these haggling tips.

"When buying souvenirs, you're more likely to get a good deal for a cash sale. If you can offer foreign currency, it may shave a little more off the price. Carry a wodge of your home currency if you plan to buy expensive items and see if the lure of US dollars or euros can get you a good price."

Joe Bindloss, travel writer

★ **The basics**

The art of haggling is based on mutual cheekiness. The shopkeeper will offer a price that is too high; the buyer will counter with a price that is too low, and the game ensues. Start by offering 60% of what the seller is asking. They'll make a show of being horrified, and come back with a price that's a little lower than their starting price. You can then go back and forth until you reach a price that's mutually acceptable.

★ **Knowing when to haggle**

There's little point trying to haggle if you see price labels, or the shop says 'fixed price'. Bargaining tends to be reserved for markets, street stalls and souvenir shops. That said, souvenir shops may be willing to give a discount for a big purchase, so there's no harm in asking.

★ **The 'walk away' trick**

If the game is set and you're still not getting the price you were hoping for, try walking away. The shopkeeper may have a sudden change of heart and accept a lower price than they'd like rather than making no sale at all.

★ **Haggling manners**

If you get to a price you've offered, it's bad form to pull out of the deal, or try to reopen negotiations on the price. Don't be too mercenary about getting a bargain – shopkeepers have to make a living, and the amount you're haggling over might make more difference to them than to you.

★ **The bundle**

If you can't get a great price on a single item, see if the seller will offer a discount if you buy a few more items. So long as they make a fair profit overall, they may be willing to offer a bulk discount.

Be an ethical spender

Travel is a two-way process – local people need to get something from the experience too. Here are our top tips for ensuring your money does some good while you travel.

Use ethical operators

When you arrange an activity or look for a guide, go with a local wherever possible. People are much more likely to give tourists a warm welcome if tourism helps them make a living. If you make all the arrangements from somewhere else, your tourist dollars may also be staying outside the area.

Stay in eco-friendly accommodation

Your accommodation spend can make a big difference, but check out the claims of eco-hotels before you stay, as not all are as green as their promotional materials suggest. Look for hotels that use renewable energy sources, recycle water, grow their own food and use reclaimed materials in construction. Staying somewhere that doesn't use any electricity or heating earns bonus points.

Shop local

Skip chain stores and supermarkets in favour of local markets, street stalls and small neighbourhood shops. It's the best way to make sure your money stays in the community, benefiting local people, while the produce often comes from the immediate area, meaning low food miles.

Eat local

Skip the chain restaurants and fast-food franchises and support small, independent restaurants, street-food stalls, food trucks and cafes. Seek out places to eat that serve local dishes (the food miles will be lower) and support local producers. If you see a place specialising in regional cuisines, give it your support to help keep food traditions alive.

Choose your souvenirs

If you're buying souvenirs, look for items made in the local area, by local people. Avoid souvenirs made from unsustainable materials, and anything made from shells, bone, feathers, fur or other parts of animals (particularly endangered species). Seek out fair-trade shops and shops run by charities and non-governmental organisations, selling products made by disadvantaged groups or communities.

Sorting out travel troubles

No trip is 100% hassle-free. Here's how to deal with three of the most common travel nightmares.

CAN'T GET A SEAT?

Can't get a seat on the flight? Try the train or the boat – it'll be slower, but there's more likely to be last-minute availability. No luck on the trains or ferries? Try the bus – multiple operators often compete on the same route, so you stand a better chance of finding a seat. Be open to alternative routes; if there's no space from town A to town B, can you get there via town C? If buses let you down, consider chartering a vehicle and driver; shared between several people, the costs can be manageable.

MISSED YOUR FLIGHT CONNECTION?

A lot depends on whether it's your fault, or the airline's. If you're connecting through to your final destination on the same carrier, they're responsible for getting you there on another flight. If you're changing airlines, or just got there late, it's at the discretion of the airline. If you're courteous and make a good case, they may book you on a later service for free; alternatively, you may be able to pay a 'rescue fee' to secure a seat on a later flight. If being late was outside your control – there was a train strike, for example – your travel insurance may cover it.

LOST YOUR PASSPORT?

If you lose your most important travel document, report the loss or theft to the police and get a police report, then contact your embassy, high commission or consulate. They can cancel your old passport and issue an emergency travel document to get you home (usually for a fee, and only valid for a specific route), or assist with applying for a new passport from abroad. Bring passport photos when you visit the embassy, plus copies of your credit cards, driving licence and other ID. You may have to contact the local authorities to replace your entry visa so you can exit the country.

THE TRAVEL HACK HANDBOOK

DESTINATIONS

India

India tells a story like no other. Nowhere else delivers so much drama and so many new experiences alongside so many challenges. Here are some tips to help you get more from the wonderful subcontinent.

Learn how to haggle

India is one place where you need a good poker face to get a great deal. Haggling here is an art form, so practise with small souvenir purchases to get your hand in before you try for the big stuff.

Read up on religion

You'll understand a lot more of the things you see if you read up on the customs, rituals and taboos of Hinduism, Islam, Buddhism, Sikhism and Jainism, and learn how to respectfully visit the holy places of these diverse faiths.

WHAT TO READ

★

Lonely Planet's *India* guidebook

★

Midnight's Children by Salman Rushdie

★

The God of Small Things by Arundhati Roy

© MILOSK50 / SHUTTERSTOCK

Be prepared for begging

Be ready with a plan for dealing with the challenges of begging. Whether you give or not is a personal matter, but you are likely to make more difference by giving to a community charity than by handing out money in the street.

See national parks humanely

Visit India's amazing national parks on foot, or by jeep or boat, rather than riding on elephants, which can cause serious damage to these giants. You'll see as much wildlife without the cruelty.

Go veggie?

Many travellers drop meat from the menu while in India to reduce the risk of stomach bugs. We'd suggest a compromise position – go veggie for street food and cheap canteen meals, and save the meat dishes for more expensive restaurants with higher hygiene standards.

Drop a class on the trains

When you cross the subcontinent by train, travelling in comfortable 2-tier or 3-tier AC class (or even fan-cooled sleeper carriages) brings a rewarding chance to interact with local people, for a much lower fare than first class.

Eat with your hands

Going *sans* cutlery (as locals do) will soon grow on you as a way to engage with India's wonderful cuisine. Clean your hands with soap or antibacterial gel, then mix rice and sauces into a ball with your right hand, and push it into your mouth with your thumb.

Have a toilet plan

We'll spare you a description of India's public conveniences, particularly those in the bazaars. Find a better class of toilet in upmarket hotel lobbies, or international restaurant chains.

Find the busy street-food stalls

To experience India's street food safely, find the busiest stalls, serving food you can see being cooked in front of you. Start with fried snacks such as samosas, which are blasted in hot oil before serving, killing off any germs.

Ask for a discount

Listed hotel room prices are more like guidelines in India. Always ask if a discount is available, particularly at quiet times. Even if you don't end up paying less than you planned, you may get a better class of room for the price you were originally quoted.

Use prepaid taxis & autorickshaws

Look out for prepaid stands for taxis and autorickshaws at train stations and airports. You'll pay a fixed fare to your destination in town, with prices posted on a list at the station.

Be wary of the plumbing

Indian hotels often have plumbing problems; before you agree to stay, check the toilet flushes, the taps and pipes don't leak, and that hot water comes on demand.

Don't tolerate harassment

Sadly, India has a sexual harassment problem – watch for wandering hands in crowds, and if you feel men are encroaching on your space, loudly protest and let public shame deter them.

Get a temple blessing

You'll probably have a temple blessing pressed on you, and a donation is expected, but don't hide away from the experience. The dab of coloured powder on your forehead is harmless – but decline *prasad* (sacred food) as it may not be hygienic.

Spending power

EXPENSIVE IN INDIA
★ Entry fees for top sights (for foreigners)
★ Alcoholic drinks
★ The cost of scams

GREAT VALUE IN INDIA
★ Mid-range accommodation
★ Fabulous street food
★ Travel by train

COSTS YOU CAN'T AVOID

★ Tips in bars and restaurants
★ Car rental (unless you're just sticking to big cities)
★ State sales taxes of 2.9–7.25%

USA

Everything is bigger in America, so they say, and that's often true of the prices – but not always. With some shrewd travel hackery, you can get more bang for your bucks every time you visit the US, and still see the best of the 50 states.

Use your points

There's nowhere better to earn and use points for flights and hotel stays, so bring the right credit cards, loyalty-scheme memberships and frequent-flier cards. For road-trip motel stops, the Choice Hotels (choicehotels. com) loyalty programme covers numerous sub-brands.

Tip – & tip generously

Service staff are paid tiny wages, and tips are vital to top up their earnings, so waiters and bar staff will firmly remind you if you fail to leave the appropriate amount. Around 15% used to be the norm, but this is creeping up to 20% or higher – ask a local if you feel unsure how much to leave.

Understand the scale of the US

US states can be as big as some countries, so be realistic about the distances you can cover. Travelling coast to coast by road will take a good week of driving all day, every day. For longer trips, a flight may be easier (choose budget carriers like Southwest to cut fares).

Rent a small car

Save by renting a compact car with good fuel economy, and whittle down your costs further by buying rental insurance separately online, or check the coverage through your credit card.

Use the back roads

For better scenery, swap interstate highways for back roads – from classic drives like Route 66 to backcountry routes such as the Natchez Trace Parkway through the South. Find more scenic drives at scenicbyways.info.

Resist fast food

Don't let the lure of cheap fast food distract you from sampling America's hearty, local cuisines. Seek out locally run diners and roadhouses, and mom-and-pop restaurants in small towns.

Get a national parks pass

The 'America the Beautiful' pass from the US National Parks Service (nps.gov/planyourvisit/passes.htm) provides free entry to more than 2000 areas of federally administered recreational land, for 12 months for just US$80.

View state forests & national monuments

View quieter and cheaper natural wonders by visiting state forests and grasslands (fs.usda.gov), state parks (stateparks.com), national monuments (morethanjustparks.com) and lands administered by the Bureau of Land Management (blm.gov).

Visit small towns

Your money will go further away from the big cities on the East Coast and West Coast. Try exploring the *Back to the Future*-style small towns of the Midwest, rural South or Pacific Northwest.

Put Washington DC on your itinerary

Normally, the national capital comes with a mark-up, but Washington DC is famous for freebies. Topping the list are the 19 free-to-browse museums (and one zoo) that make up the Smithsonian Institution, covering everything from art to aviation.

Dive into America's legends

Immerse yourself in the national story at the revolutionary monuments of Philadelphia and Boston, the federal monuments of Washington DC, and landmarks linked to modern cultural icons, such as Elvis Presley (Graceland in Memphis).

Be part of America's reimagining

The US is engaged in a national process of self-reflection over its history – participate at sights such as the Legacy Museum in Montgomery, the National Civil Rights Museum in Memphis, and the Jim Crow Museum of Racist Memorabilia in Big Rapids.

Use farmers markets

The best and freshest food in the US comes from the land, so seek out regional farmers markets in agricultural areas, such as California's Napa Valley and Sonoma, and urban foodie enclaves like NYC, Seattle, San Francisco and Santa Fe.

WHAT TO READ

★

Lonely Planet's *USA* guidebook

★

A Walk in the Woods by Bill Bryson

★

Blue Highways by William Least Heat-Moon

Spending power

EXPENSIVE IN THE US

★ Food-truck meals

★ Gasoline

★ Passes for city transport, national parks and more

GREAT VALUE IN THE US

★ Hotels, particularly in big cities

★ Organised tours

★ Train fares

Australia

Getting it right down under can take some planning, as there are huge distances to cover, lots of amazing (and pricey) travel experiences, and a few unwelcome surprises in the undergrowth. Here's how to get the best from Oz.

Consider domestic flights

Distances in Australia are continent-sized – travelling overland from Perth to Sydney involves an epic 3900km (2400-mile) drive on rutted desert roads. It's easier to let planes take the strain for cross-island trips and save driving for the coast.

Respect Aussie customs

Australia has some of the strictest quarantine laws in the world, so avoid importing anything made from plants or animals, including fruit, vegetables and items made from wood, leather and feathers.

WHAT TO READ

★

Lonely Planet's *Australia* guidebook

★

Picnic at Hanging Rock by Joan Lindsay

★

True History of the Kelly Gang by Peter Carey

Tips are voluntary

Australian restaurant and bar staff receive fair wages, and tipping is optional. If you get great service, feel free to leave 10%, but staff won't feel slighted if you don't.

Pace your drives

Inland roads in Australia are often monotonously straight and ruled by the heavy freight trucks known as road trains. Pace your drives with regular stops to fend off fatigue – you'll usually find a country pub every two hours or so.

Drive off-road

Australia is one of the best places in the world to test your off-road driving skills. Start off gently by taking a rented 4WD along the designated beaches that are open to drivers at Fraser Island, or be more ambitious on the challenging Birdsville Track or the Telegraph Road to Cape York.

Go with an Indigenous Australian guide

If you plan to properly explore Australia, let the land's original custodians guide you. Aboriginal-run tours operate all over the country, offering a chance to support Indigenous communities and learn about the land from the people who know it best.

Be critter conscious

Read up on Australia's dangerous spiders, scorpions, bush ticks, fish, toxic seashells and other nasties.

Australian Geographic's *Australia's Most Dangerous Animals* book is good reading before you lift your first toilet seat...

Swim safely

Sharks and crocs are out there, but don't overlook the annual migration of poisonous box jellyfish on the north and east coast from November to May. Always ask locals whether it's safe to swim before you go in.

Be wildlife-aware

Many Australians avoid driving at night in rural areas because of the wildlife on the roads. Take care around dusk, when kangaroos and other marsupials loiter roadside.

Sample the wine

Aussie wines are legendary, so grab a copy of Clive Hartley's *Australian Wine Guide*, book a tour with transport, and raise a glass! The best, most accessible wine trails are the Barossa Valley and McLaren Vale near Adelaide; the Yarra Valley and Mornington Peninsula near Melbourne; the Hunter Valley near Sydney; and Margaret River near Perth.

Stay in national park campgrounds

National park campgrounds in Australia are an experience. They're plentiful, inexpensive, and come with toilet blocks and sometimes solar showers and barbecues – and you'll feel like

Dr Doolittle as the wildlife comes out to investigate you at sunset.

Slip, slop, slap

Do as locals do in the sun: slip on a shirt, slop on some sunscreen and slap on a hat. For the beach, pick up a rash shirt or wear a sun-blocking layer of clothing.

Get a Greyhound pass

The Greyhound Australia Whimit Pass is a bargain. You can get 30 days of unlimited bus travel on the east coast for A$265 (US$180), or go Aussie-wide over 120 days for A$369 (US$250).

Learn the local vernacular

Aussie English has its quirks. Grab a secondhand copy of Lonely Planet's *Australian Phrasebook* and you'll know if someone is complimenting or dissing you.

Spending power

EXPENSIVE IN AUSTRALIA
★ Organised tours
★ Fine (and even not-so-fine) dining
★ Domestic flights

GREAT VALUE IN AUSTRALIA
★ Hostel accommodation
★ National park visits
★ Bus transport

Thailand

Thailand is the easy way into the Far East – fun, friendly and fabulous in all the right ways, and as well-suited to a beach break as a spiritual retreat at a forest monastery. Here's how to get maximum grins from the Land of Smiles.

Respect the king, or else

Lèse-majesté – disrespecting the king or royal family – is a criminal offence, so be respectful and avoid defacing any image of the king (for example, on a banknote). It's usual, though not enforced, to stand silently when the national anthem is played before the movie in cinemas or in the street at 8am and 6pm.

Be wary of sleaze

Thailand's sex-tourism trade can lead to hassle for ordinary tourists in places such as Bangkok, Phuket and Pattaya. Be wary of bars with pink or red lights, scantily clad female staff and a clientele of non-Thai men, and be ready to fend off approaches from sex-workers.

Know the drug laws

As well as the death penalty for importing drugs, Thailand has tough penalties for possession of hard drugs, including in party locations such as Ko Pha-Ngan. Conversely, cannabis has been decriminalised and can be bought in licensed shops.

Drink wisely

Alcohol is expensive and it's only licensed for sale from noon to 2pm and 5pm to midnight, though the post-lunch ban isn't strictly followed by hotels and restaurants. There are also dry days for major Buddhist holidays. Make your money go further by sharing a bottle of Thai whisky and mixers with friends.

Visit many monasteries

Thailand's *wats* (Buddhist monasteries) are gleaming wonders, dripping with statuary, murals and gold, and most are free to visit, so fill your spiritual boots. Make some inexpensive offerings of gold leaf, incense or lotus blooms and experience *wats* the way locals do.

Take the train

Thailand's trains are clean, calm and well-organised, and a bargain for long trips, such as the Bangkok to Chiang Mai run, particularly in second-class sleeper berths. Make bookings easily online via 12Go.Asia.

Motorcycle safely

Plenty of inexperienced riders get injured on rented motorcycles and scooters in here. Only hire a bike with proper insurance, and ride slowly and defensively, giving way to larger vehicles.

Know the local taboos

Never disrespect a Buddha image by pointing your feet towards it or touching it on the head (something also inappropriate for people). Monks are forbidden from coming into contact with women, so don't touch a monk or pass them something directly.

WHAT TO READ

Lonely Planet's *Thailand* guidebook

Sightseeing by Rattawut Lapcharoensap

Bangkok Wakes to Rain by Pitchaya Sudbanthad

© LOVELYPEACE / GETTY IMAGES

Feast on street food

Thailand rivals India for the world's best street food, so take advantage. Ask locals for the must-try regional dishes and the location of the best night markets – they usually set up around 4pm, serving everything from pad thai to rice bowls and satay sticks.

Be kind to elephants

Elephant rides are offered all over Thailand, but it harms these creatures. Visit camps that offer the chance to walk with, feed and wash retired logging elephants instead – such as Chiang Mai's Elephant Nature Park.

Avoid dodgy tuk-tuk rides

Tuk-tuk drivers are notorious for taking tourists on unrequested detours to commission-paying shops and dubious 'massage' parlours. Insist on being taken where you want to go, or use the GrabTaxi app to summon a hassle-free rideshare taxi instead.

Stay with five stars

Thailand's five-star hotels are a bargain compared with most other countries. If you fancy a stay in a room with a private butler and room service from a dozen restaurants, Bangkok could be the place to do it.

Spending power

EXPENSIVE IN THAILAND
★ Alcoholic drinks
★ Imported Western foodstuffs
★ Tours by longtail boat in Bangkok

GOOD VALUE IN THAILAND
★ Street food
★ Guesthouse and hostel stays
★ Dive courses in Ko Tao

Egypt

Egypt has wonders – and travel challenges – to spare. Try these tips before you head home thrilled by the sights but lumbered with a carpet, an onyx pyramid and a full brass table service for six that you never knew you needed.

Be baksheesh ready

The concept of 'baksheesh' spans everything from begging to tips for finding you a seat on a busy train, but don't feel obliged to hand out cash on demand. Tip if someone is genuinely helpful, or if you feel they are in need, rather than simply because they ask.

Be a smart customer

The owners of Egypt's souvenir shops are famous for their skills of persuasion, but don't be talked into spending more than you planned for. If you feel the sales pressure becoming

WHAT TO READ

Lonely Planet's *Egypt* guidebook

Palace Walk
by Naguib Mahfouz

The Yacoubian Building
by Alaa Al Aswany

© DAN BRECKWOLDT / SHUTTERSTOCK

uncomfortable, walk away, despite the shopkeeper's protestations.

Cross the desert conscientiously

Before you agree to a trip by horse or camel at ancient sights such as the Pyramids of Giza, check that the animals are healthy and well cared for – if your mount looks thin and tired, go with another operator.

Beat the queues at the Egyptian Museum

The crowds at Cairo's Egyptian Museum can resemble Ramses II's funeral procession. For a less busy experience, avoid Fridays, when many local families come. Arrive before opening time (or immediately after lunch), and leave your bag (and camera, if you can live without taking photos) at the hotel for quicker security checks.

Travel respectfully

Egypt has some conservative attitudes, especially away from the big cities, so follow local cues on dress: cover arms and legs, respect that women should cover their hair at religious sites, and keep beachwear for the sand or hotel pool.

Beat the heat

Temperatures in Egypt can be incendiary in summer, with daytime highs exceeding 40°C (104°F). Defeat the heat by

getting up early for sightseeing, or going out in the mid-afternoon as temperatures are starting to dip. Picking a hotel with air-con should go without saying.

Respect the seasons

The biggest crowds gather during the cooler winter season, when you'll need a warm layer for the cooler evenings. For a quieter experience, come from March to May or in September to early October for temperatures that are still below the summer peak.

Visit an oasis

There's nothing quite like visiting a real Egyptian oasis, and our pick is Siwa, by the Libyan border. It's the real deal, complete with ancient ruins, verdant palms and saltwater pools where you can dive in for a Dead-Sea-style float.

Explore with a guide

A guide can make the ruins of ancient Egypt come alive, but be wary of dodgy would-be guides making your acquaintance near the sights. Seek out licensed, accredited guides who actually know their hieroglyphs.

Take a boat trip on the Nile

Taking a *felucca* ride on the River Nile is a timeless experience, so long as you arrange it carefully. The classic route travels from Aswan to Edfu over three days, but check what's included and confirm the price before you set off – toilet

tents are useful; blankets and a sunshade are essential.

Get the best from the Red Sea

Bring your own mask and snorkel to Sharm el Sheikh, Hurghada and Dahab – there are spots where you can go in off the shore without paying for an organised diving or snorkelling trip. Give space to potentially dangerous marine life, such as sharks, lionfish and spiny sea urchins.

Explore the Nile's west bank by pedal power

The west bank of the Nile in Luxor is home to the Valley of the Kings, but there's plenty more to explore. For a less crowded experience, rent a bike in Luxor and cycle around quieter sites, such as the Colossi of Memnon, made famous by Shelley's *Ozymandias*.

Spending power

EXPENSIVE IN EGYPT
★ Entry fees for top-tier sights
★ Imported foodstuffs
★ Alcoholic drinks

GOOD VALUE IN EGYPT
★ Food in local restaurants
★ Red Sea diving
★ Travel by train

COSTS YOU CAN'T AVOID
★ High city-centre prices
★ 15% service charge at restaurants and bars
★ Steep VAT of up to 20%

France

Sophisticated France is rich in culture, steeped in history, filled with romance and always has a delicious meal waiting at the end of the day. But challenges await in the world's most visited country, from strikes to food prices – stay one step ahead with these tips.

Learn some French
At home, the French prefer to speak their own language. You'll have an easier time if you master the basics (or at least enough to order a coffee and croissant).

Get a Paris pass
Save on sightseeing in pricey Paris with the Paris Pass (parispass.com), covering free entry to top museums and sights for two to six days – just make sure you visit enough sights to justify the cost (look out for discounts online).

Avoid August
The French go on holiday en masse in August, and many businesses close – much to the chagrin of foreign visitors. Wait until September, when locals get back from their hols.

See the museums (while you're young)
France's commitment to culture extends to free entry to museums for under 18s and citizens of the

European Economic Area aged 18 to 25. Not European? Flash your student card – the International Student Identity Card (isic.org) is widely recognised.

Drink free water with meals

Waiters tend to assume tourists want to pay for mineral water with every meal. If you're happy with tap water, simply ask for a *carafe d'eau* and save a few euros.

Eat prix fixe

Be on the lookout for *prix fixe* (fixed price) menus, which offer big savings over ordering courses separately. For more quality cheap eats, seek out busy Arabic and North African neighbourhoods, such as Marseille's Noailles.

Watch your pockets

Many big French cities have a pickpocket problem, particularly around tourist sites and on public transport. Keep your valuables secure and your bag closed.

WHAT TO READ

★
Lonely Planet's *France* guidebook
★
All the Light We Cannot See by Anthony Doerr
★
Les Misérables by Victor Hugo

Avoid road tolls

Many French Autoroutes (highways) are also *péages* – toll roads where you'll have to make regular payments to complete your journey. Set your SatNav to 'avoid tolls', and you'll be routed to free but slower routes.

Beware La Grève

True to their revolutionary past, the French go on strike often – a headache for travellers. Monitor the airwaves for news of upcoming industrial action, and avoid public protests, which can turn into battles with the police.

Stay in aires

Opting for *aires* – free (or low-cost) roadside mobile-home stops – is a lifesaver if you're going long-distance with a campervan or mobile home. Find them all over in Alan Russell's *The Best Aires in France 2023/24*.

Have a picnic

Nowhere does picnic ingredients quite like French markets. A fresh baguette, a wedge of *fromage* (cheese) and some charcuterie is all you need for a gourmet al fresco meal at the park.

Savour French wine wisely

When exploring wine regions such as Bordeaux, Burgundy and Champagne, travel from vineyard to vineyard on an organised wine tour, or by bike, to stay on the right side of strict drink-driving laws.

Or just grab a good bottle...

If you're looking for a quaffable *bouteille du vin*, check the capsule (the metal foil around the cork). Green is reserved for superior Appellation d'Origine Contrôlée/Protégée wines, and the letter 'R' (Récoltant) signifies that the wine was bottled by the person who grew the grapes – another marker of quality.

Travel by TGV

The French rail network is world class and trains are fast, frequent and reasonably priced. Connect in on international services such as the Eurostar (eurostar.com), then book as you travel at sncf-connect.com, or use the excellent Interrail/Eurail Pass (interrail.eu).

Spending power

EXPENSIVE IN FRANCE
★ Supermarket groceries (for self-caterers)
★ Accommodation in big cities (particularly Paris)
★ City centre parking

GOOD VALUE IN FRANCE
★ Wine – obviously!
★ Picnic ingredients from markets
★ Brilliant bread from the local boulangerie

Turkey

Some say Turkey is the eastern end of Europe, others the gateway to the Middle East. Either way, it's overflowing with wonders. Here's how to immerse yourself in its brilliant beaches, ancient ruins, fine food and Islamic soul.

COSTS YOU CAN'T AVOID

★ İstanbul prices
★ 18% VAT on goods and services
★ Service charges added to the bill in posh restaurants

Celebrate the kebab

The ubiquitous kebab is just the beginning of the carnivorous adventure in Turkey. Every region has its variations, from İstanbul's Beyti (spiced ground meat in filo pastry) to minced meat and aubergine Patlıcanlı kebabs in the south. Graze Turkey's ocakbaşı (grill) restaurants and become a kebab connoisseur.

Experience it differently during Ramadan

Travel can be disrupted during the Muslim fasting month of Ramadan; if you come during the

WHAT TO READ

★
Lonely Planet's *Turkey* guidebook
★
The Bastard of Istanbul by Elif Shafak
★
The Museum of Innocence by Orhan Pamuk

fast, head for the coast where rules are more relaxed. Avoid driving at sunset, when locals rush home for the first meal since sunrise.

Grab a Museum Pass

Turkey's Museum Passes (muze.gen.tr/MuseumPasses) offer discounted entry to top museums around the country, but you'll need to make plenty of museum trips to justify the recently hiked prices. Scope out options using the Museums of Turkey app.

Respect Turkish culture

Beachwear is fine for the sand in Turkey, but people tend to be more conservative away from the resorts, particularly in the north and east. Once you leave the beach, wear clothing that covers the legs, chest and upper arms. When entering mosques, women should cover their heads, remove shoes and stick to areas set aside for women.

Learn of three big empires

The ancient Greeks, Romans and Ottomans all left their indelible mark on Turkey – be sure to visit the sites they left behind. İstanbul, Bursa and Safranbolu are top for Ottoman treasures, while the best Greco-Roman ruins – Ephesus, Termessos and friends – dot the Mediterranean shore.

Be ready for beach tar

Beach tar washed up from shipping lanes can be a menace on Turkey's beaches. If you plant your foot on a blob, remove the tar with a rag soaked in baby oil or a paste of baking soda and water.

Know the law

As well as a strict ban on drugs, the export of antiquities is prohibited, even if purchased in good faith. It's also forbidden to insult the Turkish nation, or its founder, Kemal Atatürk; save political discussions for the privacy of your hotel room.

Don't get caught out by winter opening hours

Many historic and cultural sites close a few hours earlier during the quieter, colder winter months, and some remote sites are completely unstaffed in the low season; always check sites are open before you visit.

Avoid problem zones

A decades-long conflict between Turkish security forces and supporters of Kurdish autonomy rumbles on in the southeast of the country. Heed travel warnings about areas to avoid and be cautious around potential terrorism targets, such as İstanbul's Taksim Square.

Clock the blocked sites

Many websites are banned or restricted in Turkey, including Facebook, Twitter, YouTube, PayPal and booking.com, so don't rely on the net. If you use PayPal, try accessing your account via the not-yet-banned mobile app.

Dress for the weather

Summer highs of 40°C (104°F) are not unheard of on the coast, but winter can be bitterly cold in central areas such as Cappadocia, so dress appropriately.

Be alert for natural disasters

Earthquakes, floods and wildfires are all potential risks, so monitor hurriyetdailynews.com and other local media sites for reports. If you get caught up in disaster, follow official advice and leave the affected area as soon as you can.

Spending power

EXPENSIVE IN TURKEY
★ Western-style coffee shops
★ Taxi rides (unless the driver uses the meter)
★ Peak-season price hikes on the coast

GOOD VALUE IN TURKEY
★ The fabulous food (particularly quick kebab lunches)
★ Domestic flights on budget airlines
★ Long-distance bus transport

South Africa

Everything in South Africa is larger than life, from the magnificent megacities and life-affirming landscapes to the teeming wildlife in more than 20 national parks. Here's how to avoid any pitfalls in Africa's southern gateway.

Fly into Jo'burg

Start your trip in Johannesburg rather than Cape Town. International flights are cheaper, and you'll be well placed to explore the national parks and reserves in the north and east.

Be shark aware

Seeing a great white is one of South Africa's top thrills, but it's best to have something between you and the shark. Heed local advice about the safe places to swim and surf, and seek out beaches with lifeguards and marked swimming areas.

Drive like a local

The key road-safety rule: keep car doors locked and windows closed while driving, to reduce the risk of carjacking. Be extra careful at night – robberies at traffic lights are common – and drive around obstacles in the road without stopping (it may be a trap).

Hit the shoulder seasons

Tourist sites get rammed during Christmas and the school holidays, but the spring and autumn shoulder seasons hit the sweet spot. Wildflowers bloom on the west coast from September, while June (late autumn) opens the whale-watching season in the Western Cape.

Take guided city tours

Wandering around the streets can be risky in big cities, so join a guided walking tour to navigate safely. Prioritise themed walks angled around historic neighbourhoods, townships and the anti-Apartheid movement, over predictable 'top sights' tours.

Connect with South Africa's struggle

Learn more about South Africa's fight for freedom at sites such as Jo'burg's Apartheid Museum, Nelson Mandela's former prison on Robben Island (staffed by one-time inmates), and Cape Town's District Six Museum.

Self-drive on safari

For the Big Five without the big price tag, rent a vehicle and drive yourself, rather than joining an organised safari. Kruger National Park can be reached from Jo'burg in four hours, with budget lodges and hostels as an alternative to luxury safari camps.

Explore vegetarian options

Away from cosmopolitan cites such as Cape Town, seek out local veggie dishes: *chakalaka* (spiced vegetables), pap and relish (maize porridge with tomato sauce), samp and beans (pounded corn kernels with sugar beans), and vegetable sauces at Indian-run restaurants.

WHAT TO READ

Lonely Planet's *South Africa* guidebook

Long Walk to Freedom by Nelson Mandela

Cry, the Beloved Country by Alan Paton

Embrace the braai

Self-catering can save you a wedge of rand, particularly if you're a natural-born carnivore. Most guesthouses, apartments and homestays provide access to a braai pit where you can barbecue to your stomach's content.

Drink the water

In most of the country, tap water is potable, so you can skip bottled and ask for tap water in restaurants. This breaks down a little in rural areas, so check with a local before drinking from the tap.

Get a Wildcard

If you plan to go big on safaris, the SANParks Wildcard pass (sanparks.org/wild_new) covers entry to more than 80 parks in South Africa and neighbouring nations for a year, but you'll need to clock up a few park visits to make savings.

Claim back your tax

If you make a big purchase in the Republic, keep the receipt – you can claim back VAT on spendings of more than 250 rand at South Africa's international airports on departure, but leave extra time for the formalities.

Follow the wine routes

Discover South Africa's rich wine heritage on a guided wine tour from Cape Town – seek out smaller, family run vineyards, such as Boschendal and Spier.

Spending power

EXPENSIVE IN SOUTH AFRICA

★ Organised adventure activities
★ Accommodation in Cape Town
★ Peak holiday prices

GOOD VALUE IN SOUTH AFRICA

★ Food, particularly for carnivores
★ Local beers and wine
★ Renting a car (compared with organised tours)

Argentina

Argentina offers a thrilling journey through captivating cultures, life-changing landscapes, sophisticated cities – and mountains of steaks. Here are some tips to help you travel the length of this great country without a hiccup.

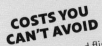

COSTS YOU CAN'T AVOID

★ Expensive inbound flights (due to lack of competition)
★ VAT of 21% or higher
★ Unpredictable inflation

Feast on the streets

To keep a lid on your budget, graze Argentina's delectable street food. Must-tries include *empanadas* (stuffed savoury pastries), *choripán* (spicy sausage baguettes), and *lomito* (grilled steak) and *Milanesa* (breaded meat cutlet) sandwiches.

Dance authentic tango

Experience real tango at Buenos Aires' local *milongas* (dance clubs) rather than touristy shows. Try Milonga Parakultural at Salon Canning (parakultural.com.

WHAT TO READ

★

Lonely Planet's *Argentina* guidebook

★

My Fathers' Ghost is Climbing in the Rain by Patricio Pron

★

In Patagonia by Bruce Chatwin

ar) or take one of the weekend classes at La Glorieta in Parque Barrancas De Belgrano.

Eat like a vegetarian

There's plenty of veggie food in meat-loving Argentina if you know where to look. Chow down on vegetable and cheese *empanadas*, pizzas and pasta, spinach-and-egg *tarta* and grilled Provoleta cheese.

Be crime conscious

Crime is concentrated in the big cities. Keep valuables hidden, be vigilant for pickpockets and bag-snatchers, and avoid walking alone at night. Beware of the spilled sauce scam, where a thief spills something on your clothes and then robs you while 'helping' you clean up.

Stay away from politics

Protests in Argentina can turn violent, so give political gatherings a wide berth. Monitor the local media for potential hot spots – *Buenos Aires Times* (batimes.com.ar) is a reliable English-language news source.

Pay a fair taxi fare

Taxis are known for hiking prices, so stick to licensed cabs and insist the driver uses the meter. Or you could order a rideshare through Uber or Cabify – you won't make a huge saving, but the price is fixed and you can share the details of the journey for peace of mind.

Hike from El Chaltén

To immerse in Patagonia's awesome landscapes, head to the trekking hub of El Chaltén – many routes can be hiked in a day without paying for a guide or entry fees. The elchalten.com website has helpful hiking info.

Be altitude-aware

Many roads and hiking trails in Argentina climb above 2500m (8200ft), including the ascent of Mt Aconcagua. To reduce the risk of Acute Mountain Sickness (AMS), climb slowly, take rest days, and consider taking Diamox tablets to reduce symptoms.

Drive Ruta 40

Legendary Ruta 40 runs offers astounding views of the Andes for 5194km (3227 miles) from Punta Loyola to La Quiaca. Parts of this high-altitude route can be driven in a conventional hire car, but you'll need a 4WD for unpaved *ripio* (gravel) sections.

Carry photo ID

You'll need photo ID (ideally your passport) when making purchases by card in Argentina, so keep yours handy – just not so handy that thieves can get at it (use a pouch hidden under your clothing).

Get more from Iguazú Falls

Visiting Iguazú Falls, South America's most famous waterfall, from the Argentine side brings you closest to its thundering power.

Jump on the first bus from Puerto Iguazú (at around 7am) to reach the viewpoints before the hordes.

Use the SUBE card

For hassle-free trips on buses, subways and trains in Buenos Aires and other big cities, grab a rechargeable SUBE card (argentina.gob.ar/sube) from a local *kiosco* (convenience store). Tap in and out on trains to avoid being charged the highest fare.

Respect siesta time

In much of Argentina, shops and businesses shut down in the afternoon while staff enjoy a siesta before reopening in the evening. If you have urgent business, do it in the morning!

Spending power

EXPENSIVE IN ARGENTINA
★ Imported goods (buy clothes and tech before you come)
★ Buenos Aires living
★ Rental cars

GOOD VALUE IN ARGENTINA
★ Filling street food
★ Budget airlines for cross-country flights
★ Bus travel through dramatic landscapes

INDEX

CONTRIBUTORS

Angela Devaney
With her partner, Graham, Angela is one half of Mowgli Adventures, sharing the love of overlanding and how to go about it.

Bradley Mayhew
Bradley is Lonely Planet's mountain master, writing about the world's most rugged hiking destinations, from Yellowstone National Park to Everest Base Camp in Nepal.

Celeste Brash
Prolific Lonely Planet writer Celeste splits her time between guidebook trips to Asia, the Pacific and the Americas and farming sustainable pearls in Tahiti.

Dan Mobley
Dan is the global corporate relations director for global beer and spirits giant Diageo, travelling all over the world to meet distillers and brewers.

David & Linda Holland
Veteran travellers Dave and Linda set up retiredandtravelling.com to spread the message that adventure has no age limits.

Janine Eberle
Former Lonely Planet editor Janine now puts her language skills to use in her adopted hometown of Paris.

David Marshall
David is a London-based e-learning expert and the CEO of workplace training company Marshall E-Learning Consultancy, specialising in diversity and inclusion.

Doug Rimington
Musician and photographer Doug started his travel journey as part of Lonely Planet's IT team.

Dr Deb Mills
Dr Deb is one of Australia's top experts on travel health, sharing advice through her Brisbane clinic and thetraveldoctor.com.au.

Duncan Garwood
Duncan is a veteran expert on Italy for Lonely Planet, also teaching English to Italian students in his home city of Rome.

Elizabeth Lavis
Travel writer Elizabeth writes about the Americas and destinations worldwide for Lonely Planet and online and print magazines.

Hugo Van Vondelen
Hugo is a rail travel specialist at Eurail, whose round-Europe train tickets have launched many young people on their first adventures.

Imogen Hall
Child therapist Imogen is an expert on travel with children, and formerly Lonely Planet's in-house family travel specialist.

Kevin Raub
Italophile Kevin has written for more than 100 Lonely Planet guidebooks, as well as contributing to *Rolling Stone Magazine*.

Laura Lindsay
Laura is a former member of the Lonely Planet family, now steering online strategy for flight experts Skyscanner.

Mark Elliott
Travel writer Mark specialises in the world's tougher travel destinations.

Mark Smith
Mark is the expert voice behind the Man in Seat 61 website (seat61.com), one of the top online sources for information on global train travel.

Matt Kepnes
Award-wining blogger Matt has spent years spreading the love of travel through his globe-trotting website nomadicmatt.com.

Melissa Hie
Foodie and avid techie Melissa set up the blog girleatworld.net to share her love of food and travel.

Mariellen Ward
Award-winning travel blogger Mariellen divides her time between Canada and Rishikesh in India; find her at breathedreamgo.com and indiaforbeginners.com.

Richard Hammond
Richard is a writer, filmmaker and founder of greentraveller.co.uk, with news on green travel trends.

Sarah McPherson
BBC Wildlife Magazine features editor Sarah is an authority on everything from birding in Colombia to Asiatic lions.

Scott Mayerowitz
Scott is the head of editorial at The Points Guy, America's leading online experts on cards, points and rewards.

Stuart Butler
Stuart is one of Lonely Planet's keenest outdoors enthusiasts.

Tom Hall
Tom is a globe-trotting cyclist and vice president of Lonely Planet.

Tom Masters
Tom is a former writer for the *Moscow Times*, and a long-term contributor to Lonely Planet, covering everywhere from Mexico to Russia and North Korea.

Trent Holden
Australian writer Trent is a prolific contributor to Lonely Planet.

Virginia Maxwell
Long-term Lonely Planet writer and editor Virginia is an expert on Turkey and the Middle East.

Published in November 2023 by Lonely Planet Global Limited
CRN 554153
www.lonelyplanet.com
ISBN 9781837580613
© Lonely Planet 2023
Printed in Malaysia
10 9 8 7 6 5 4 3 2 1

General Manager, Publishing Piers Pickard
Senior Editor Robin Barton
Editors Karyn Noble, Polly Thomas
Layout Designer Jo Dovey
Picture Research Ceri James
Print Production Nigel Longuet
Cover Illustration © Muti

Written by Joe Bindloss: Joe is Lonely Planet's former destination editor for South Asia, and the writer of more than 70 Lonely Planet guidebooks and reference titles, covering everywhere from Nepal to Madagascar. He also contributes regularly to newspapers and magazines, including the Telegraph, Guardian, Evening Standard and National Geographic Traveller.

STAY IN TOUCH lonelyplanet.com/contact

Lonely Planet Global Limited
Digital Depot, Roe Lane (off Thomas St), Digital Hub, Dublin 8, D08 TCV4 IRELAND

Paper in this book is certified against the Forest Stewardship Council™ standards. FSC™ promotes environmentally responsible, socially beneficial and economically viable management of the world's forests.